"You'll feel the tension facing the first fem̶[...] stration acrobatics Thunderbird pilot. Yo[...] nurse corps officer to be appointed as commanding officer of a medical surgical unit as she treated the severely wounded in Iraq. You'll admire one of the first women to attend the naval academy and then smile at discovering that her family became the first in America to send every member to the naval academy. After reading *Changing the Rules of Engagement*, you'll feel renewed pride and patriotism in the U.S. military and the sacrifices of these women."
—Jane Hampton Cook, author of *Resilience on Parade: Short Stories of Suffragists and Women's Battle for the Vote*

"Most of us from that pioneer generation of women in defense have been too busy to stop and take notice of how far we've come in the last thirty years. With *Changing the Rules of Engagement* Martha LaGuardia-Kotite has given us the chance to do so, and the journey is indeed wondrous to behold."
—Kathleen Troia "KT" McFarland, former national security official in the Nixon, Ford, and Reagan administrations

"Full of journeys that must be shared. I'm so glad that Cmdr. Martha LaGuardia-Kotite has made it her mission to delve into the personal stories of seventeen trailblazers and share them with all of us."
—From the foreword by Rep. Debbie Wasserman Schultz (D-FL)

"Will surely serve to inspire future generations of young women to follow in their footsteps and achieve excellence in our nation's armed forces."
—From the foreword by former representative Jeff Miller (R-FL)

CHANGING THE RULES OF ENGAGEMENT

Inspiring Stories of
Courage and Leadership
from Women in the Military

CHANGING THE RULES OF ENGAGEMENT

Martha LaGuardia-Kotite

FOREWORDS BY
Rep. Debbie Wasserman Schultz
and
Rep. Jeff Miller

With a new afterword by the author

Potomac Books
An imprint of the University of Nebraska Press

For those who have served.

Contents

Acknowledgments

I am fortunate to have a family of supporters and friends who sustain me by their encouragement. Instrumental from the beginning were my coauthor of *My Name Is Old Glory* (2012), Trish Marx; Toni Kotite; Ellie Roy; Amy Goodpaster Strebe; Tina Burton; Sue Ross; the incredible Andy Ryan; Brig. Gen. Wilma L. Vaught, USAF (Ret.); and Lt. Col. Marilla J. Cushman, USA (Ret.), at the Women in Military Service for America Memorial Foundation, Inc.

I cannot imagine a better reviewer of my drafts than Bruce White. Many thanks to my agent, Colleen Mohyde of the Doe Coover Agency; and Elizabeth Demers, my editor at Potomac Books, for believing in this book from the first conversation.

There are many others to whom I am grateful for making themselves available and assisting me with various requests, from lining up approvals and interviews to sharing background information, suggestions, photographs, and continued assistance. I especially thank the public affairs officers and enlisted members of the U.S. Army, U.S. Air Force, U.S. Navy and Marine Corps, and U.S. Coast Guard who were instrumental over the course of several years in the development of this book.

For all the women who served in the military and by their example made this book powerful and possible (and to the men who believed in them and held open the door), I am most indebted to those who agreed to share their stories with me: Marene Allison; Capt. Sue Bibeau, USCG (Ret.); 1st Sgt. Brenda R. Chrismer; Vice Adm. Vivien S. Crea, USCG (Ret.); Sharon Disher; Lt. Col. L. Tammy Duckworth, USA (Illinois National Guard); Gen. Ann E.

Dunwoody, USA; Capt. Gina Harden, USN; Lt. Col. Nicole Malachowski, USAF; Col. Pam Melroy, NASA, USAF (Ret.); Capt. Catherine D. Florenz Michaud, USMC; Capt. Maureen M. Pennington, USN; 1st Sgt. Debra A. Sharkey, USMC (Ret.); Master Sgt. Bertha Thompson, USA; Brig. Gen. Paula G. Thornhill, USAF (Ret.); Command Master Chief Mattie M. Wells, USN; and U.S. Air Force veteran Rep. Heather Wilson. Special thanks to Rep. Debbie Wasserman Schultz and Rep. Jeff Miller for recognizing the service of veterans and acknowledging their courage and contributions.

Finally, my thanks and love to my husband, Peter Kotite, for his enduring support; my sons, John Kotite and Aaron Bruner, for being constant inspirations and beloved companions; and my mom, Martha LaGuardia, for always believing in my bigger dream.

Foreword

Rep. Debbie Wasserman Schultz (D-FL)
Chairwoman, Democratic National Committee

Our brave women and men in uniform proudly perform one of the toughest jobs in America—protecting our freedom—often risking their own lives in the process. This is an unfathomable concept for most of us, but our members of the armed forces preserve and protect an ideal so much bigger than any one person. They do it with courage and a willingness to make the ultimate sacrifice, which makes each of them remarkable in their own special way.

Changing the Rules of Engagement is an anthology full of journeys that must be shared. I'm so glad that Cmdr. Martha LaGuardia-Kotite has made it her mission to delve into the personal stories of seventeen trailblazers and share them with all of us.

What comes through in each woman's story is the courage it took to knock down the barriers in her way; the struggles that made her stronger and taught her more about herself and made her the leader she is today; and the dogged determination that would not let her consider failure as an option.

Like so many others in this book, I was raised by incredibly supportive parents who taught me that I could grow up and achieve anything. I believed them. After all, I was born in 1966—the era of women's empowerment. I never knew a time when there weren't women in public office. My parents always taught me that women could reach for the stars. Just a few years later, America witnessed Sally Ride literally prove them right. But it wasn't always that easy.

Many of these women are Women of Firsts: the first female Thunderbird pilot, one of the first women to pilot a space shuttle mission, and the first woman to graduate from the Naval Academy with a degree in systems engineering. There was no one who came before them to show them the way. They had to be the ones to decide how to shatter the glass ceilings and make it possible for women after them to follow suit and break even more new ground.

Changing the Rules of Engagement shows the reader how each woman evolved as a leader and learned from her mistakes along the way. We can all relate, yet we're also in awe of these amazing women. Their work ethic and guiding principles are rooted in their military training and have been a credit to their successes in civilian fields as well—from politics to small business to parenthood.

As Pam Melroy describes when talking about her journey to becoming an effective leader, she had to learn from her missteps and refine her leadership style over time in order to inspire others and see effective results. Her best advice is simple, yet rings true, no matter the field: "Being honest and naturally adjusting to complement the situation is key." Another featured woman is Command Master Chief Mattie Wells, a woman after my own heart when she talks about a commitment to working hard and getting it right so that people know they can count on you to get the job done.

Many of these women didn't necessarily set out to make a name for themselves. They were simply following their passion, and because of that they were able to reach new heights and end up in the history books. Though they may not have realized it at the time, each of these women has broadened the scope of possibilities for future generations. Today our children are seeing more women in prominent, nontraditional jobs held by women who have come before them. It is my hope that by the time their children are looking around for career inspiration, it won't be such a novelty to see a female CEO of a Fortune 500 company or even a female president of the United States. Rather, they will believe that their goals can be limitless because women can achieve anything to which they aspire—and it will be proven true again and again.

The feats you'll read about in these pages are not impressive simply because a woman accomplished them—they are staggeringly brave and interesting *human* stories. In her book *You Learn by Living*, former first lady Eleanor Roosevelt wrote, "You gain strength, courage, and confidence by every experience in which you really stop to look fear in the face. You are able to say to yourself, 'I have lived through this horror. I can take the next thing that comes along.' You must do the thing you think you cannot do." *Changing the Rules of Engagement* is about courageous women who did just that, and then some.

This book celebrates the stories of inspiring, successful women in the U.S. military who blazed a trail for the generations yet to come, with the hope that they would carry the torch. The determination these women possess to get the job done, and to do it better than ever, is something I hope people take away from this book. As women, we cannot fail because we allow ourselves to be outworked and we can't ever give up. Their journeys show us what it really means to be an exceptional woman who is changing the rules of engagement. No matter what path you have chosen or what stage of life you find yourself in as you read, you will glean wisdom from these pages.

Foreword

Rep. Jeff Miller (R-FL)
Chairman, House Committee on Veterans' Affairs

The blessings of liberty enshrined in our Constitution and enjoyed by all Americans would not be possible without the selfless dedication of our service members and veterans. These brave individuals put their lives on the line so that we may be free. Their heroism is celebrated in our national anthem, and we should honor their service and sacrifice every single day of the year. As chairman of the House Committee on Veterans' Affairs, I have the honor and privilege of working with our nation's veterans and service organizations on a daily basis. I believe it is imperative to honor and support our nation's service members and veterans in every possible way. But sometimes it can be difficult to fully appreciate the commitment and bravery of certain segments of our armed forces because their accomplishments far too often fail to receive the full recognition that they deserve. As Martha LaGuardia-Kotite points out in her aptly named book *Changing the Rules of Engagement,* the extraordinary accomplishments of female service members—who had to break down barriers and virtually change the rules of engagement to overcome obstacles and reach the pinnacle of military service—cannot be diminished.

LaGuardia-Kotite served our nation for more than twenty years in the U.S. Coast Guard, and this firsthand knowledge gives her the perfect background to recount the stories of the seventeen female service members interviewed in the book. LaGuardia-Kotite's interviews help to shine light on some of the outstanding accomplishments of our female service members. The interviewees range from astronauts to admirals and include a lieutenant general and a former congresswoman. LaGuardia-Kotite's interview subjects demonstrate the kind of courage and honor that typifies our military and makes it the most elite force in the history of the planet.

Changing the Rules of Engagement: Inspiring Stories of Courage and Leadership from Women in the Military helps strengthen my belief that we should honor our service members and veterans every day of the year. LaGuardia-Kotite and the women she interviewed will surely serve to inspire future generations of young women to follow in their footsteps and achieve excellence in our nation's armed forces. This book will also help Americans appreciate the commitment and service of our veterans and inspire us to extend our most sincere gratitude to all our service members and veterans every day. Let us never forget it is their service and sacrifice that form the unshakable foundation on which the freedom of our nation rests.

Prologue

During my rewarding ten years of active duty and twelve years as a reserve officer in the U.S. Coast Guard, I was perplexed by the undercurrent of negative perceptions cast upon women serving in the armed forces by both the public and some members within the ranks of the free world's greatest military in the dawn of my career. After graduating from the United States Coast Guard Academy in 1989 and going off to sea, first on a cutter and then a patrol boat, I was asked many questions: Why did you join the service? Are you a lesbian? What's it like working in a man's world? Did you get the plum patrol boat executive officer assignment because you were the token example for other women?

I believe these questions stemmed from a lack of understanding as to why women choose the military as a way of life, a profession. The fact that it can be a career choice offering superior education and leadership training does not seem to be widely appreciated. One reason for these misconceptions and persistent stereotypes is limited interaction with military women, who have been few and far between. Even I was not accustomed to serving with another woman. As of the close of 2011 (according to Women in Military Service for American Memorial Foundation, Inc.), active duty women made up 6.8 percent of the U.S. Marine Corps, 15.7 percent of the U.S. Coast Guard, 13.6 percent of the U.S. Army, 16.4 percent of the U.S. Navy, and 19.1 percent of the U.S. Air Force—14.6 percent (214,000 women) across the armed forces of 1.47 million active duty volunteers. Adding the reserve and the guard, women make up an additional 15.5 percent (73,000) of this 471,000-person force. Even though women in the military are given gender equality when it comes to pay, unlike the corporate workforce, promoting based on potential continues to be a challenge, as is the slipping progress for women in America's workplace.

The inspiration for this book occurred in 2006 when I was a panelist for an academy women symposium at the Women in Military Service for America Memorial located in Arlington, Virginia. I was invited to talk about my corporate career after leaving active duty and my experiences writing my first award-winning book, *So Others May Live: Coast Guard's Rescue Swimmers: Saving Lives, Defying Death.* The discussion was being held in a darkened room at the end of a hall. Dimly lit memorabilia of women who had died in the Iraq and Afghanistan wars were displayed. While waiting for the audience to walk down and the lights to come up, I was drawn to a folder containing a single page with a photo and a few lines describing the lives of each woman who had given the ultimate sacrifice for our freedom. It occurred to me that these beautiful service members had died too young. Some were teenagers, some were in their twenties, and a handful were in their thirties. Had they died before getting married or finding a true love? Had they had a chance to experience being a mom? Had their lives even permitted them the opportunity to build up anxiety about turning thirty, owning a home, or balancing career and family? Had wrinkles of maturity started to add character around their eyes? Did their dreams come true?

While in the quiet of that room, teary-eyed because of what I had learned, I committed myself to help bring recognition to the inspiring service of military women. The power of the emotion I felt at that moment for those who had died for their country while serving in career fields that had at one time been exclusively filled by men, along with the knowledge that a book about the evolution of women's military service would honor those who served, captured my heart. I was driven to write a book acknowledging the spirit and leadership of the forerunners who broke the military's equivalent of the glass ceiling. I knew from my own experience that many Americans had no idea of the extent of these assignments or realized that today's military women serve in combat-related roles. Progress was attained slowly and painfully. Women made trade-offs and sacrifices to adapt to their work environment while keeping their authenticity in a predominantly male world, and by doing so they became catalysts for changing the rules of engagement.

Changing the Rules of Engagement: Inspiring Stories of Courage and Leadership from Women in the Military documents the face of female possibility as seen through the lives of seventeen women who have broken barriers or performed extraordinary feats that sometimes required the changing of policy, law, and even culture in the traditionally male-dominated military. What I found during my interviews with these women, whose careers span from the 1970s to present, was that many of the perceptions that I experienced in 1989 when I was a junior officer still existed in 2011. Twenty years ago, my roommate, Annie Ignacio, and I were the first women ever assigned aboard our ship, the USCGC *Resolute*, with a complement of twelve officers and crew of sixty-eight enlisted men. While aboard the 210-foot cutter, we were immediately viewed as bad luck due to maritime lore and considered less than capable by some of the crew who had never served with a female. The wives were threatened to see their husbands set sail for months with two female ensigns and excluded us from social events and the then all-important Officers' Wives Club while in homeport. These attitudes were not passé even by the 1990s, and challenges of respect remain for some women who go to sea or serve even today.

The media certainly has had its share of stories about women who were sexually harassed or assaulted, compounding the military's image problem. Such scandals as the 1991 Tailhook and the 2003 Air Force Academy sexual assault investigations highlighted the need for a change in climate. Unfortunately, the press and military authors rarely celebrated women whose exemplary service and leadership on the battlefield date back to the American Revolution and whose service in the U.S. Armed Forces began in 1901. It was these early veterans who emerged attempting to break new ground and pushing for changes in rules, policy, and warrior culture to accept women as valued members of the military. The stories of women whose courage and dedication afforded them adventurous careers while serving their country and whose passion for education and learning equaled their desire for opportunities to serve as leaders in a way that enabled them to give back to their country were rarely acknowledged.

In the pages that follow, I have done my best to write about the perspectives and recollections of the women I interviewed, who all served from the 1970s to today. Their views are their own and do not necessarily represent the views of the Department of Homeland Security and the U.S. Coast Guard, or the Department of Defense and the U.S. Army, U.S. Navy, U.S. Marine Corps, U.S. Air Force, and the guard or reserves. It is my hope that sharing the aspirations and accomplishments of these women in uniform will lead to a greater appreciation of the contributions made by women in the military and inspire others, both men and women no matter what phase of life they are in, to follow their example and dream a bigger dream.

1

Out of This World

Col. Pam Melroy, NASA, USAF (Ret.)

Being an astronaut is soup to nuts an amazing, wonderful,
fabulous experience on every level.

Driven. That's how Pamela Ann Melroy, age fifty, came to describe her career.
But, it was not until she was older and had achieved her dream of becoming a National Aeronautics and Space Administration (NASA) astronaut that
she could reflect and truly understand this about herself. She admitted that
"driven" was the word her parents, husband, and best friends would use, too.
"It takes a long time to understand who you are relative to other people,"
says Melroy. "As far as I'm concerned, I'm perfectly normal. I'm right in the
middle of the road on everything. But I'm obviously not." She laughs.

Far from being in the middle of any road, Melroy, from the tender age of
ten, knew she wanted to be an astronaut. The explorer Ferdinand Magellan,
who led the first circumnavigation of the globe in the early 1500s, wrote "unlike the mediocre, intrepid spirits seek victory" over the seemingly impossible:
"It is with an iron will that they embark on the most daring of all endeavors
. . . to meet the shadowy future without fear and conquer the unknown." With
an iron will Melroy drove toward her passion and became qualified as a space
shuttle pilot in 1996, one of the most daring of all endeavors. In fact, she was
one of only three female pilots to fly the NASA space shuttles.

Until they were retired in 2011, space shuttles were used for carrying
astronauts to the International Space Station (ISS) and other destinations in

low-Earth orbit, such as the Russian Mir space station and the Hubble Space Telescope. NASA built five of these space-worthy orbiters designed for reuse. They were capable of routinely launching into orbit using disposable rocket boosters, which provided the energy and power necessary to lift them out of Earth's gravity into space. Crews conducted scientific research and helped deploy or repair satellites and built the ISS. The vehicle that carried the people and payload to orbit later returned them to Earth as a glider.

Construction of the ISS, more than four times as large as the Russian Mir space station, began in 1998. The ISS measures 356 feet across and 290 feet long with almost an acre of solar panels to provide electrical power to six state-of-the-art laboratories. Sixteen nations—Brazil, Canada, Japan, Russia, the United States, and eleven nations of the European Space Agency—contributed to the scientific and technological resources to establish this unprecedented, complex laboratory in orbit, critical for research capability. According to ISS press materials, the research conducted aboard ISS would lead to discoveries in medicine, materials, and fundamental science to benefit people all over the world—and serve as an indispensable step in space exploration.

Melroy launched on her first flight from the Kennedy Space Center in Florida on October 11, 2000, aboard *Discovery*. Six American astronauts and one Japanese astronaut were on board what was the fifth U.S. mission to the ISS. Their objective was to rendezvous and dock with the ISS so they could deliver modules to expand the space station in preparation for its first resident crew, using *Discovery*'s robotic arm and performing four spacewalks to configure the Z1 Truss and Pressurized Mating Adapter 3. The mission was accomplished in 202 orbits, for a total of 5.3 million miles during thirteen days in space.

Melroy again rocketed into orbit on October 7, 2002, this time serving as the pilot of the *Atlantis*. The crew returned to the ISS for another assembly mission, delivering and installing the third piece of the station's eleven-piece Integrated Truss Structure. Three spacewalks were required to outfit and activate the new component. Melroy also acted as the internal spacewalk choreographer. This mission was accomplished in 170 orbits, totaling 4.5 million miles. The crew returned to the Kennedy Space Center after ten days.

Nearly four months later, *Columbia* was lost during its return to Earth on February 1, 2003. Melroy's experience and leadership prepared her to participate in one of the most significant events of her life. She was called upon to help with the *Columbia* Reconstruction Project Team as the lead for the crew module reconstruction. "In the military we take it for granted that there's going to be an investigation, but usually not by people from the same unit, especially if it was a fatal accident," she told me. "Of course we didn't have that luxury. At NASA, we were the only ones."

It was deeply personal for Melroy to be a part of the team that reconstructed *Columbia* and storyboarded the events of the last flight in order to understand how the crew died and what lessons could be learned. The cause of the *Columbia* accident was not known. The Reconstruction Team at the Kennedy Space Center reassembled the vehicle from pieces of debris picked up where they fell in Texas and Louisiana and laid them out in their relative orientation "to see if we could find the smoking gun," according to Melroy. "In fact, the Reconstruction Team did find the smoking gun—evidence that there had been a breach in the leading edge of the left wing." The seven-member crew devoted sixteen days to research. The joint effort between the NASA Accident Investigation Team (NAIT) and the *Columbia* Accident Investigation Board (CAIB) resulted in a final report which indicated that during ascent "a sizeable piece of debris struck the left wing of the *Columbia*" eighty-two seconds after launch. The debris was insulating foam, which had shed from the shuttle's external tank—the fuel tank that feeds the shuttle's main engines on ascent. On-orbit reviews of the flight found nothing unusual with any of *Columbia*'s systems; there was no indication of the damage that had occurred on ascent. Upon reentry into the earth's atmosphere, *Columbia*'s damaged wing allowed hot gas generated from the friction of the descent to infect the internal wing area. Over Littlefield, Texas, a small town near the Texas–New Mexico border, *Columbia* began to lose tiles from the damaged wing one minute prior to final disintegration. The breach provided a pathway for hot gas to intrude further, "leading to extreme heating and thermally induced strain" and eventual "loss of vehicle control leading to aerodynamic breakup."

During the reconstruction, Melroy was in charge of a separate room with limited access to the pieces of the crew module that were not causal factors in the accident. Personal effects and training equipment were identified and used to learn as much as possible about how the crew died. Though unrelated to the cause of the tragedy, this information could help answer questions that would make human spaceflight safer in the future. How did their equipment perform? How comprehensive was their training? Were there lessons to be learned? Around her every day were the broken pieces of the *Columbia* crew module. "I could see the stories emerging. Why did this come back the way it did? The debris was talking to us."

Melroy was a natural choice to serve as the deputy project manager for the crew survival investigation. As the technical manager, overseeing the engineering portion of the review, she worked with the medical deputy and a team of more than thirty engineers. NASA published the *Columbia* Crew Survival Investigation Report containing the results from the team's findings in 2008.

Melroy launched from Kennedy Space Center for the last time as a NASA astronaut on October 23, 2007, aboard the space shuttle *Discovery* with a crew of seven. The trip would take fifteen days, bringing Melroy's career total to thirty-eight days in space. She served as mission commander, responsible for the crew's safety and delivering "Harmony," a node 2 element that opened up the capability for future international laboratories to be added to the ISS. The crew was also tasked with relocating the P6 solar array to the portside of the Integrated Truss Structure.

While docked to the ISS, the crews of the ISS and *Discovery* were unfurling the solar array when a panel snagged and ripped. The situation was immediately alarming and dangerous. "We had a huge problem. It was really, really bad," said Melroy. "The seriousness of the problem required both crews to drop everything else we were doing to try and work on the solution." Three days of intense focus were needed to figure it out. They decided to send a spacewalker out on a combination of two robotic systems attached to each other, which could extend farther than any single robotic arm, in order to reach the solar array.

The solar array was fully powered and could not be turned off. If Scott Parazynski, the spacewalker, touched it while stitching up the panel, the array's 120 volts DC would shock and potentially injure him or damage the suit. "It was really nerve-racking for me to see him out there all the way," said Melroy. "I personally coordinated the spacewalk from inside because of the danger involved." She talked directly with Scott on the radio as the events took place. In conjunction with excellent work from the robotic arm operators, Dan Tani and Stephanie Wilson, and the other spacewalker, Doug Wheelock, the crew was able to complete the repair. Scott Parazynski and Doug Wheelock came back inside after a seven-and-a-half-hour spacewalk.

Later in the mission, Melroy and the first woman to command the ISS, Peggy Whitson, were in the space station lab. They had business to discuss. Soon Melroy would be undocking the orbiter from the space station with great ceremony on board both vehicles. "We had our toes hooked underneath the foot rail and were just sort of bobbing as you do in zero gravity," Melroy said. "She had a cup of coffee and I had tea while we talked about the planned ceremony and what we had just gone through together." It was a wonderful memory of a significant experience they shared—both the problem and the resolution. "The fact that both of our teams had thrown everything they had at it to solve it and how well it had gone . . . we sort of were basking in the success of that together." According to Melroy the success resulted in one of the most famous mission "saves" in the space shuttle program.

For the little girl who without any doubt in her mind knew she was going to be an astronaut one day, this rendezvous in space with another woman astronaut was far-fetched. "If you had said to me when I was eleven years old that not only are you going to be a woman commander and at the same time in space you are going to meet up with a woman commander of the space station, and you guys are going to hang out, I'd say, 'No way!'" exclaimed Melroy. "It just happened by accident. It's not like somebody said, 'Let's do this for a publicity stunt and have Pam and Peggy in space at the same time.'"

Women astronauts did not exist in 1972 when Melroy chose her career. Born in 1961, she was in high school when women's liberation and the feminist movements were gaining momentum, and there was a lot of talk about what women could do. "There were a lot of mixed messages about being well behaved and being lady-like. At the same time this idea that you can do anything you wanted to do existed," Melroy said. Fascinated by the sky, she loved astronomy. She spent a lot of time thinking about the great things she could do and discover in the universe beyond Earth. The idea of being an explorer appealed to her. Interested in science, Melroy knew she could learn new things and be an explorer through scientific research.

In 1969, the world was awestruck when the history-making Apollo program launched the first men to the moon. Neil Armstrong and Edwin "Buzz" Aldrin took one small step out of the *Eagle* landing craft for man and one giant leap for mankind. "It completely captured me," said Melroy, who talked with her parents about exploring space. "My parents were great. They really put their money where their mouth was and never said there was something I couldn't do." With the support of her parents and the career experience of her father, who had served in the U.S. Air Force, she felt comfortable joining the same service and taking a giant step leading to a career in space. "All the astronauts I heard of were military jet pilots. I said, 'Well, I guess that's what I'm going to do.' At that time, when I made my decision, women were not even allowed to fly jets in the military."

According to a historical timeline provided by the Women in Military Service for America Memorial Foundation, each military service had its own pace for permitting women to into new fields and combat related operations. The first navy women to earn wings as military pilots did so in 1973, and it was in 1983 when the first navy woman completed Test Pilot School. In fact, when the U.S. military sent service members to Grenada in 1983 for Operation Urgent Fury to evacuate and protect the Americans there and extinguish a communist threat, approximately two hundred army and air force women were part of the operation serving as air crew, military police, and transportation specialists. Yet it was not until 1993, when the secretary of defense lifted a ban restricting women from fighter pilot training, that they were guaranteed flying jets into combat.

As progress was being made for women to serve in roles previously exclusive to men, Melroy graduated from Bishop Kearney High School in Rochester, New York, in 1979. Melroy went to on to study at Wellesley College, a top-ranked educational institution and women's college in Massachusetts. While there, she majored in physics and astronomy and was a member of the U.S. Air Force Reserve Officer Training Corps (ROTC) detachment at the Massachusetts Institute of Technology (MIT). "One of the values of a single-sex education, especially for women, is that, well, every physics major that I knew was a woman," said Melroy. "The idea that women weren't good scientists or just couldn't do science was ludicrous to me."

After receiving her bachelor of science degree in 1983 and being commissioned through the U.S. Air Force ROTC program that same year, Melroy became a graduate student at MIT and earned a master of science degree in earth and planetary sciences in 1984.

Melroy left academia for air force pilot training at Reese Air Force Base in Lubbock, Texas, where she graduated in 1985. For the next six years she flew the KC-10 Extender, an air refueling and airlift tank, as a copilot, aircraft commander, and then instructor pilot. She flew more than two hundred combat and combat support hours for Operation Just Cause, the 1989 U.S. action in Panama; Desert Shield, the United States' August 1990 response to the Iraqi Republican Guard's invasion of Kuwait; and Desert Storm, in January 1991.

The transition from MIT student to air force pilot was eye opening for her in many ways. There were many cultural issues she came to understand as she continued to develop her leadership style as a young lieutenant and captain. She discovered during her ROTC years she had a passion for leadership, not only the intellectual challenge of strategic and tactical thinking, but also the idea of team building and relationships. People in the academic environment thought her aspiration to be an astronaut was cool and had no issues with it; in fact, many of her peers also wanted to be astronauts. "I wasn't prepared for the occasional derision I would get going into the air force," she admitted. "Usually the second thing you learned about me after my name was that I was going to be a military test pilot and an astronaut." There were a lot of reactions. Some were very supportive of her goals, but some pilots she trained with as a junior officer felt that the highest aspiration she should have was to be a pilot in the air force. "'What do you mean? You're acting like this is just a stepping-stone to some other job you want.' There were some issues like that. I had to learn that my Pollyanna, bright-eyed, totally focused and driven attitude could sometimes be annoying and not popular with everyone," she said. "I think it was a great opportunity for me to learn about human nature."

Melroy wanted to be a good leader. She knew that she needed to understand how different people were going to react to different stimuli. It was hard, but she tried to learn from every experience and didn't focus too much on callous comments. "It was tough being a woman. Your credibility was not very high. You had to prove yourself all the time," she said. As a matter of routine she tended to treat the incidents as funny experiences, such as the time her KC-10 squad deployed to Oman. Melroy, her copilot, flight engineer, and boom operator had flown together for years; they were all good friends. But the boom operator, in high demand to augment other crews who were shorthanded, had to stop flying temporarily because he had flown more hours than was legal.

As a result, Melroy was introduced to a boom operator from a different unit who was going to be flying with her crew on a mission. During the preflight briefing she remembered thinking that the boom operator was trying to challenge her competence as a pilot, even though at this time in her career she was a senior instructor and was training aviators to fly the KC-10. She recalls thinking, "*Oh yeah, that's how they treat you when they're not really sure if you're a good pilot*. It was entertaining to me. This guy was feeling things out a little bit, trying to see what he could have on me, whether he could push me. He was clearly ambivalent." She used one of her favorite lines when he said he'd never flown with a woman: "I said, 'I've flown with lots of guys. So I'll show you the ropes.'" After the flight, on the bus ride back to the hangar, she could tell that he had put her into the category of "an exception."

The same kind of test would happen again at Edwards Air Force Base. In June 1991 she attended the one-year U.S. Air Force Test Pilot School at the California base. After graduation, Melroy was assigned to the C-17 Combined Test Force, assessing the capability and new designs of the air cargo and supply ship as a test pilot until her selection for the astronaut program. Going into this new role, she had a substantial amount of experience and a proven record as a skilled pilot, so if there were a problem, it was most likely owing to the jet and not the pilot. "Being a test pilot is like doing experiments with airplanes. It's just so cool," said Melroy. "You think about all the things that might happen. The safety process takes you through all the mitigation and you can understand the engineering behind the handling qualities and structures." She planned test missions and went out to fly them with a level of freedom she did not experience in the operational environment. "There's nothing more fun than to jump into a new aircraft," Melroy said. Plus there was a huge chunk of airspace to work with during the experimenting. As a test pilot she flew in more than fifty different aircraft. She used this experience to create a database of the aircraft in her mind to help solve problems that would develop or to prevent problems in developmental aircraft for the next generation.

Edwards Air Force Base was very different from her previous assignments. There were not many women, and the C-17 contractor test pilots were a lot older, including many Vietnam War veterans. It was a definitely a "mature" flying environment. She fondly recalls her squadron commander at Edwards, who was African American and familiar with breaking barriers, as a great leader. Lt. Col. George London set the stage for her to win a level of acceptance with her unit early on. To do so, her skill as an individual would be tested during a dramatic in-flight experience.

She had said to London that she'd like to get qualified as an air refueler—someone who can successfully hook up and conduct a fuel transfer from the tanker providing fuel to the C-17 while in flight. This difficult operation involves precision flying and a steady approach. The aircraft to receive fuel, in this case the C-17, would approach the tanker from below and behind—a complex task requiring a slow, gradual narrowing of the distance between the two aircraft. The tanker would then insert a flying boom, or tube, into a relatively tiny receptacle on top of the C-17 aircraft to make the connection and begin the transfer of fuel. If either the tanker or the receiver determines that aircraft separation is required immediately to avoid a mid-air collision, an emergency breakaway or detachment procedure is ordered.

"I didn't really know that there were basically only three people certified to fly air refueling in the whole unit. Several pilots had tried to get certified and had been refused," said Melroy, who only learned of this after her test flight for certification as an air refueler. London took her up in a C-17. As she pulled up behind the tanker to attempt to refuel she thought, *I used to teach people how to do this, I'm all set.* Seconds later, she called, "Breakaway, breakaway, breakaway," before conducting an emergency disconnect of the fuel nozzle connecting the two planes in mid-air and pulling up and away from the tanker without a mid-air collision. "Holy cow! On my very first approach I had to call a breakaway. I had probably had that happen three or four times in my entire six-year career in KC-10s, and it was never because I had screwed something up," she said. "I could tell my approach was too hot. I was not in control."

The pressure was on. She was the test pilot in the unit and the woman. She reset her mind to forget it, drive on, compartmentalize, and go back in, learning from the experience. She and London talked about it, debriefed, and she was ready to try again. She did get connected, got some gas, and backed out. Three more times she practiced it successfully and thought, *They'll probably be scared to death to have me do this without supervision.* What she didn't know was that she had done as well as anyone had been able to with the tricky maneuver. When they got down on the ground London said, "Okay, that's it. You're signed off." She cherishes this memory of the trial and tribulation of qualifying in a field not many aviators had successfully completed because London allowed her an opportunity to prove herself early on with something that was technically challenging, even in that environment of seasoned, war-tested pilots. "That made a huge difference to the level of acceptance that I experienced in my squadron," she said.

She found the test pilot job wonderful for the flying but stressful because of the politics and scrutiny of working in a large Department of Defense program. However, it prepared her for going to NASA in 1995, another demanding job with similar characteristics. NASA had politics, talented pilots, and mission specialists. It had developing technologies and worldwide interest in the missions. "You're doing things with a vehicle (spacecraft) that is essentially experimental. There isn't a lot of experience with it. You land for the first time on the actual day. Train as much as you want but you've got to make it right the first time you actually fly it."

Melroy worked for NASA for fourteen years. Her basic astronaut training was one and a half years. After that she was assigned a mission and focused her advanced training on that specific mission. "Being an astronaut is soup to nuts an amazing, wonderful, fabulous experience on every level," she said.

Melroy came in as a pilot astronaut, which meant eventually she was going to be a mission commander. In the history of the space shuttle program there were only three women pilots in the astronaut office: Eileen Collins, Sue Still Kilrain, and Pam Melroy. "NASA didn't hire any other women pilots." Still was the first person in their class of twenty-three astronauts to fly, and Melroy flew last. The assignment order was not based on performance. After two flights, Still left NASA following marriage to raise her children. "It's just Eileen and I, only two women who have commanded the shuttle missions. I'm a little disappointed about it," said Melroy, who'd hoped that more women would have been selected overall.

The astronaut office was a very team- and family-oriented environment, personality-driven, with a lot of support for learning. "Its really kind of a dream environment in a lot of ways because there are so many smart people; everyone is so bright, so nice, skilled, and interesting," said Melroy. "Yet it's a different leadership situation where the challenge for a commander in a lot of ways is keeping people from fighting for the hardest assignments. Astronauts all want the biggest challenge they can find." As the mission commander, she had to dole out the assignments. Somebody had to take photos, run the computers, and put the boxes away after they began to orbit. These jobs were not as glamorous as a spacewalk or robotics.

"It's the awareness that everyone has his or her part to play whether you're in the spotlight or not," said Melroy. She admired how the crew of *Apollo 11* worked together as a team for the historic moon landing. Someone had to stay behind in the command module, *Columbia,* and not walk on the moon. "Everybody's got a favorite astronaut, even astronauts have favorite astronauts, and for me there's no question: it's Mike Collins. Neil [Armstrong] and Buzz [Aldrin], landed on the moon. Mike stayed in the command module, alone, circling the moon while they walked on the surface." Melroy was inspired by his attitude and also by the amazing experience he chronicled in his book, *Carrying the Fire.* He was out of touch with the Earth, out of touch with his colleagues, and completely alone in space on the far side of the moon. She recognized that what the world remembered most about the first moonwalk was Armstrong's and Aldrin's steps, yet what influenced Melroy the most was the idea that you don't have to have the greatest, amazing experience or the hardest one to be a part of a historic team and make a difference.

Melroy's passion for leading people and learning to lead teams began when she was in ROTC. Then and now, her deeply held belief is that leadership is something you study, read about, and practice like any other discipline. "You continually evolve to higher and higher levels. The highest form basically revolves around who you are. You have to get it from within, all the elements of your personality, as opposed to anything anybody else can impose on you," she said. "You really have to tap into your own self and all the parts of yourself to be able to capture that additional range of leadership style." Your personality, she says, drives what kind of leader you are, determines your strengths, and defines your comfort zone.

After learning about human nature and how people react to each other's personalities and mannerisms, she moved on to the next level, which involved extending her leadership style outside her comfort zone. "How do I push their buttons? How do I give them what they need to inspire them or bring them together as a team?" she wondered. Each situation calls for a different style, some dictatorial and demanding, others consensus building, and still others a pep talk or simply standing back and letting people do what they do best. "If you have a certain comfort zone for how you handle things, it's just not going to be a fit for every situation." Being honest and adjusting to complement the situation are key. Melroy found the tools to do this by watching other people, her peers, the ones who were effective. "The truth is we all get angry. We all encounter a variety of situations in our family and personal lives that elicit a different response out of us. So if you can tap into that, you've evolved. My leadership style is a Pam leadership style. Not a male or female style. It's Pam. It's based on who I am, my experiences and my beliefs, my values."

Another value Melroy has lived by and holds as a core belief is the concept of service. She's lived a life of service and seen how rewarding making a difference for others, for country, can be. She feels productive when she's helping someone else. "I realize that's a very significant part of what brings meaning to your life. It's your relationships, your family and what you can do for them. They depend on you and need you. You depend on them. What a wonderful thing the military can teach you and provide an opportunity to perform that service. Not just for your family but for your whole country."

What did she sacrifice to accomplish her dream? "I think it's true that you do sacrifice things. I would say that because I set my goal and was shot straight out of a cannon right at it and didn't deviate from my plan," said Melroy. "I think what I sacrificed are the things I didn't learn by taking a more meandering path and letting things evolve. You lose some of the options for richness and depth in your life when you think in a linear way." For instance, she has always wanted to learn to speak French, and there has been no time for it. While she has no regrets, she's aware of the sacrifices she made. "People live their lives differently, and they get different things out of it based on their choices."

Melroy chose to fly and go to space when military jet pilot training was prohibited for women. When women began entering air force pilot training in 1976, Melroy was a teenager. By 1993, when women were allowed to fly as fighter pilots, Melroy had already been flying the KC-10 for years. "I was born at the right time to become a pilot astronaut, but I think the young women out there right now were born at the right time to go far beyond that and go outside of Low Earth Orbit (LEO) and hopefully command a mission to Mars." The challenge in *Apollo* was going to the moon. The challenge of Melroy's generation of astronauts was to master LEO and build the International Space Station. "The next great leap for astronauts is outside of LEO, again, not just back to the moon but on to Mars," she said. "It's about exploring our solar system and beyond. That's an enormous technical challenge that will require basically everyone. No longer in this world is it acceptable to limit the skill sets that you're picking from to half the population, in other words, the men. You have to pick from the best and pick the best of the men and women."

Melroy left NASA in 2009 as one of only three women to qualify and fly as mission commander of the space shuttle. She retired from the air force and worked for Lockheed Martin on the next generation of spacecraft. As deputy program manager, she provided engineering services to help design the space-craft *Orion* for NASA, which will take astronauts outside LEO and be used for deep space exploration.

In 2011 she decided to move closer to her family and go back into government service. She plans to work with the Federal Aviation Administration's Office of Commercial Space Transportation. The commercial space industry will allow people to pay their way to travel into space. Several companies are engaged in trying to figure out how to make that happen, and her job will be to regulate it, make it safe, and promote those opportunities for human commercial space flight. "I will get very involved in the evaluation of human elements to make sure they have those pieces squared away," she said.

Melroy often looks up toward the sky to remember where she's been and how it felt orbiting in a spacecraft two hundred miles above the Earth. She loves to go outside when there is a space station pass to look at it. At the time of our conversation in February of 2011, seeing the space station was extra special because one of her colleagues from her ROTC detachment at MIT, Cady Coleman, was on board when it passed. Melroy also got to have a video teleconference with Coleman and see her floating around up there.

"Those moments, when I see the space station pass overhead and know that Cady is there, I know what an amazing place the space station is. I know because I've been there. It's way more than looking at your pictures of the best vacation you ever had. It's really something that you have very deep, visceral memories of what it's like to live there. What it's like to float. What it's like to lose things and find them again. The sense of closeness, the camaraderie, it's a complete experience that engages every part of who you are. The memory comes back whole. You kind of mentally take a vacation and go back. That's really great."

2
Supersonic

Lt. Col. Nicole Malachowski, USAF

The number one key to success? Always surround yourself with positive people. They need to be people who believe in your dreams as much as you do. If they don't, you wish them well. You never act out of anger. You go forward with the people who believe in you and you keep that team.

What kind of guts does it take to fly the U.S. Air Force F-16 Fighting Falcon upside down, 200 feet above the ground at 1,500 miles per hour? The fastest car in the world only clocks 267.86 miles per hour, according to *Guinness World Records*. For F-16 pilot Maj. Nicole Malachowski, a member of the air force's elite aerial demonstration team, the Thunderbirds, the skill and ability to execute such a harrowing maneuver at speeds few of us will ever experience were simply part of her typical ten-hour workday. The Thunderbirds are a team made up of a dozen officers and more than 120 enlisted air force members who serve together to present precision, aerial maneuvers to exhibit the capabilities of modern high-performance aircraft. They travel all over the world to showcase the excellence embodied by American airmen. Malachowski had what it took—intelligence, stamina, and ability. It was her childhood dream to fly a military jet. Flying an F-16 in breathtaking aerobatic maneuvers, thrilling millions of spectators staring from the ground, was a bigger dream. Yet, she was scrutinized by people all around the world for being the first woman in U.S. military history to become a demonstration jet pilot. Many questioned why a woman should belong on this legendary team that had been limited to men since its founding in 1953.

The process of applying for the Thunderbirds is very competitive and selective. There are a series of interviews and candidates have to provide a letter of intent explaining why they want to become a Thunderbird. The résumé of every potential team member is reviewed as well as letters of recommendation. Malachowski wanted to apply for a simple yet modest reason, "to share the Air Force story. I saw it as a way to share the story of my friends, my peers, their families, and all of the airmen I'd met along the way. Theirs is an amazing story indeed. It was humbling to consider the thought of representing all of the dedication, professionalism, and sacrifice of those across the Air Force. I also was excited about the idea of being able to be a positive influence on kids . . . that part proved to be very rewarding." When the U.S. Air Force announced that Malachowski would perform in one of the six demonstration aircraft as right wing Thunderbird Number 3 during the 2006 and 2007 show seasons, the press and public delivered both praise and criticism of her capabilities as a Thunderbird pilot. Internet blogs and articles questioned her selection, her skill, and her ability to represent the exclusive male club. Others doubted she would succeed even before she showed up to wear the "Ambassadors in Blue" uniform, representing the pride, precision, and professionalism of America's airmen.

"Here I was living this amazing air force life. Everything good in my life had come from the air force, including my husband," laughed Malachowski. She would not have met her husband, a lieutenant colonel and weapons system officer (a "backseater" in the F-15E Strike Eagle), had she not joined the same service. "All of a sudden, I came out of that protected environment—a place where I really fit in, a place where I had been nurtured—into this global media frenzy only to find that there were people actively rooting for me to fail. These were people who didn't know me or know anything about me."

She had been assigned to the 494th Fighter Squadron, based at Lakenheath, England, when the announcement was made that she had been chosen for the Thunderbirds. She began to wonder if she had made a mistake, and there was a moment before she left England for the Thunderbird's Arizona training field when she looked at her husband and said, "I don't know what I've got myself into."

Malachowski's qualifications were not in doubt. A proven, accomplished pilot and mission commander, she had flown the F-15E Strike Eagle from 1999 to 2005. She served in three operational squadrons as a front-line fighter pilot. The Strike Eagle had a dual role with two crew members, a pilot and a weapons systems officer, performing air-to-air and air-to-ground missions at low altitude, day or night, and in all kinds of weather. The aircraft was equipped with avionics and electronic systems, which gave pilots the capability to reach a long-range target, destroy enemy positions on the ground, and return to base. She flew missions in Iraq, providing close air support during Operation Iraqi Freedom. She also had experience as an air liaison officer on the ground, embedded with the U.S. Army on the Korean Demilitarized Zone, the buffer zone between North and South Korea.

The criticism made her think twice about the challenges ahead. "People said I should have been prepared for the media attention," said Malachowski. "I say that until you've been under the media's magnifying glass for being the first to do something, it's impossible to prepare for the media frenzy that ensues." She was thankful for the air force public affairs officers who helped her navigate the maze. Inside the maze she found some people whom she appreciated because they understood that her role as the first female Thunderbird was a catalyst for discussion on the role of women in the military and on whether or not women should be in combat. Women Air Force Service Pilots (WASPs) went through this experience in WWII, and military women went through it before and after the combat ban was lifted in 1993. "It seemed to be open again for criticism for some people in late 2005."

Talking it over with her husband, Malachowski decided she would in fact join the Thunderbirds' squadron. The team welcomed her, knowing that together they would deal with the heat of the spotlight from the world press. She insulated herself with the support of her husband, family, friends, and the Thunderbird team. As the thirty-year-old buckled into the cockpit of the fourteen-million-dollar aircraft for the first time, she focused on the reason for her decision to join the team. She had dreamed of this moment since childhood. "If you can answer, who am I? What do I value? I think you can get through anything," said Malachowski.

She had five months to prepare for her March 2006 airborne debut. Once qualified she would fly the Number 3 position for two show seasons and then train her replacement. Six pilots shaped the demonstration team at each show. She trained with them in Arizona where she learned the Fighting Falcon's capabilities and how to execute breathtaking, acrobatically precise maneuvers in tight formation. "It is a lot more homework and studying than people think," she said. "It's not like the movie *Top Gun*, where you just kick the tires and light the fires." For each one-hour sortie, or demonstration flight, the team spent an hour in a formal brief, planning the mission, and another two hours debriefing. Outside of that, she said she could spend up to four hours a day doing "chair flying," "closing my eyes and visualizing the whole show, every maneuver, every radio call, every little thing my hands and feet would be required to do."

"The reason you have to plan, study, and refine your techniques as a team is because when you're up there it's not seconds that count—it's split seconds," explained Malachowski. "Flying is all about decision making and decisiveness." The evasive maneuvers pilots put the high-performance jets through are also physically and mentally exhausting. "Pulling nine Gs [nine times the weight of gravity] on your body is absolutely draining. You can pull so many Gs that you pop blood vessels in your skin. We call them 'G-measles.' You'll come back with red dots all over your body. It's not a joke—the nine-G environment is not something for the faint at heart." Physical fitness and intense concentration are also crucial to executing the mission safely. "After a Thunderbird air show I would sometimes be so tired from concentrating it was like I had run a marathon. Mentally it's very draining."

Malachowski stresses the importance of teamwork, be it flying in combat or in an air show. "It's your wingman [pilot flying behind the lead plane] carrying you and helping you out when you're having a bad day and vice versa," she said. "Flying is a dynamic environment. You have to be ready to adapt on a moment's notice in concert with the other pilot."

The wingman chemistry can make the difference for the team. Pilots in dangerous flying environments work in pairs. The two pilots train closely together and know each other's strengths and weaknesses. "If you turn the wrong way, your wingman is trained to key the microphone and ask some questions," Malachowski said. "They're trained to say, 'You know what, let's knock this off and start all over.' We're there for each other's safety and protection. I don't care if it's in an F-15E over Iraq or in a Thunderbird F-16." The heightened sensitivity to each other's performance includes an acute awareness of a slower radio call and response. If that happened, she said she'd give the other pilot a little more room. "We'd give him an extra six inches or a foot as we're going around," she said, acknowledging that she would have days like that herself. "You feed off of each other to get the whole mission done. Some days people are carrying your weight and other days you're carrying theirs. On a true team, nobody's keeping score."

The hard work and long hours were worth every split second in the cockpit. Malachowski's assignment as the first female Thunderbird was a success. Indirectly, her accomplishment furthered the career opportunities for women in the military. Most of the press coverage was positive, and she received thousands of letters from young children. "It was helpful having those kids write. I got over 4,000 letters and they were all positive," she said cheerily. "They really carried me through on some of those tougher days."

Malachowski was proud to represent the men and women of the U.S. Air Force. "I did it because I knew that I wanted to be a part of this team. I did it because I believed in the Thunderbird mission. I did it because I love my air force, and I want to tell people about it. I did it because my husband believed I could," said Malachowski. "In retrospect, it was clearly one of the most transformational three-year periods of my life. Absolutely."

She learned that "you can speak volumes without saying a word. I think when I was younger I would try to explain myself or justify myself or sometimes fight back. It's not necessary." Malachowski said she was transformed by the grace and maturity of the Thunderbird pilots who taught her how to fly the intricate maneuvers. They were supportive and helpful, knowing what she was going through. "My appreciation for that wingman concept that I learned in combat, expanded a bit more," she said. "I also learned that when you're a Thunderbird, you're an instantaneous role model, a responsibility that can not be taken lightly."

She was humbled by this enormous responsibility, one she took very seriously. It became apparent at the demonstration shows where long lines of fans and young children waited to speak with her and ask for her autograph. She felt like it was not very long ago that she had dreamt of flying. "I remember telling my dad when I was five I wanted to be an air force fighter pilot. He replied, 'You're going to be a great air force fighter pilot.' That was an important turning point," said Malachowski. "If he had said girls couldn't be fighter pilots or it's too difficult, we'd have a different story today, I'm sure of it." Now, it was her turn to be that positive influence in a young life, to be that one person who said to a child, "Yes, I believe in you. I think you're going to be a great fighter pilot, a great teacher, or a great ballerina some day," like her dad did for her. For the young girls who came to watch her fly, it was really important to see someone like her who'd had a dream and made it come true.

Malachowski grew up in Nevada in a middle-class American family, a middle child with an older brother and younger sister. Her mom stayed home with the kids until Malachowski was in high school, then took an executive secretary job at a major hotel in Las Vegas. Her dad was a successful architect and general contractor designing and selling custom homes. "My dad definitely gave me a competitive spirit. Grades were very important, as was excelling and doing your best." Her mom was more social than her dad, but both were well liked.

Her parents, she acknowledged, were very encouraging. If she had changed her mind about becoming a pilot, they would have been supportive as long as anything she did was with 100 percent effort and passion. They did not tolerate mediocrity. Their way to help her figure out how to achieve her goal was by being methodical, asking,*So, what does one have to do to become a fighter pilot?*

She did her research to find out. In junior high she learned about the U.S. Air Force Academy located in Colorado Springs, Colorado. As a seventh grader, she wrote the academy, asking for an application. She wanted to read it and be prepared. They wrote back saying she was too young to apply but provided the information she requested. From reading about how to achieve her dream, she learned that she would need to earn a college degree and become a commissioned officer. The academy offered a scholarship for the degree, and she would be commissioned upon graduation. "So the chances of becoming an air force officer and a fighter pilot were perceived by me to be best coming out of the academy. That's why I chose it. I chose it as a twelve-year-old," Malachowski said. "I was pretty maniacally focused."

Malachowski worked hard in high school to achieve an appointment to the U.S. Air Force Academy's Class of 1996. When she attended the service school for officers, things had changed quite a bit for the better for women. When the first women were admitted to military academies in the mid-seventies and well into the mid-eighties, many did not welcome their participation or presence.

When Malachowski was a freshman in 1992 she felt that the climate was positive. The number of female cadets had grown to 154, with 1,064 of her classmates being male. "Certainly we were the minority, but I did not notice anything was different about us," she said. "I had an amazing experience at the academy. I was never treated any differently. I recommend the academy to anybody, male or female, who's looking for a career in the air force."

She graduated in 1996 with a bachelor of science degree in management and a minor in French. A total of 922 cadets graduated with her, including 123 women. (Today, the total number of cadets attending the academy exceeds 4,500, more than 900 of whom are women.) Later, Malachowski studied online through American Military University while she was a Thunderbird to earn a master's in national security policy.

After her tour as a Thunderbird pilot, she became a White House Fellow—a one-year, special duty assignment working with senior White House staff members, which enabled her to retain her military rank and pay. As a fellow, Malachowski served on the Presidential Transition Support Team (PTST) at the Office of the President-Elect (OPE) and held the position of deputy chief of staff at the U.S. General Services Administration. She talked about leadership issues with other top-ranked government officials and dozens of national leaders, including President Bush and President Obama, scientists, engineers, and artists, including Placido Domingo, Nancy Brinker, and Maya Lin. Part of a team of fourteen fellows, her peers included doctors, lawyers, teachers, bankers, and scientists, and she gained firsthand experience working in the federal government and a better understanding of the process by which the nation is governed.

Following her White House assignment, the Malachowskis stayed in Washington, D.C., where she worked in the air force's Office of International Affairs. One of her main duties was serving as the chief of international developmental fighter programs for the secretary of the air force. In this capacity she developed an export policy and provided foreign disclosure guidance for F-15, air-to-ground weapons, and targeting systems. She advised foreign military and governmental officials on foreign military sales programs and prepared correspondence and briefings for senior Department of Defense and congressional members.

Over her fourteen-year career, her choices for assignments—flying the F-15, being a Thunderbird pilot, and being a White House Fellow—focused on opportunities in which she could be part of a team. "I think that when you strive to be part of something that's bigger than yourself and you strive to be part of a team to achieve a team goal, you'll find a lot more fulfillment," said Malachowski. "I try to live by that. The older I get, the more I know it's true."

She has been a keynote speaker for more than a thousand engagements. Some of these have been prestigious, such as the Women in Military Service for America Memorial. Others have been informal, such as a group of Girl Scouts or school students. When a child asks how she can have opportunities similar to hers, Malachowski says there's no recipe. "It boils down to this. Always surround yourself with positive people. They need to be people who believe in your dreams as much as you do. If they don't, you wish them well," she said slowly. "You never act out of anger. You wish them well, and you go forward with the people who believe in you, and you keep that team."

She likens her role to being team captain of her life. She picks her own players and feels children should think of their lives that way too. "They can choose positive influences. Or they can choose negative ones. It's on them. It's personal accountability and personal responsibility," she said.

Malachowski was frequently asked if she had a super-secret skill that enabled her to have such a successful career. "It's not true," she laughs. She doesn't dwell on her weaknesses, and she forgives herself for her mistakes. She tries not to get frustrated and laughs at the silly things she does like putting keys in the refrigerator or tripping over her shoelaces or forgetting to send birthday cards. She believes her success came from TLC. "Most people define TLC as 'tender loving care.' I define it as timing, luck, and circumstance. What that means though is you must be open to opportunity. You must be aware of opportunity when it comes. You must not be afraid to try to seize opportunity. The surest way never to go to the Air Force Academy, be a Thunderbird pilot, or be a White House Fellow is not to try."

Malachowski shared another tip about developing a leadership style that's true to who you are. She describes herself as a "cheerleader"—the ever-smiling, positive kind of person who stops to have a conversation with the cashier at the store. When her officer career started and she was assigned to a fighter squadron, she tried to fit in, be one of the guys. "I thought, *I'm going to act like them and be more serious. Not smile as much*," she recalled. "I tried it for six months, and it crushed me. It was draining. I was miserable. I think fewer people wanted to listen to me or follow me." People sensed she was not being herself. After this experience she learned to act naturally.

As a leader she has also realized the importance of caring about her co-workers and their families. "When you're really trying to move an organization, individualized attention as in, 'Hey, John, I remember your wife and family were coming this weekend. How'd it go?' is important," she said. Leaders need to demonstrate individualized, focused attention for their team members, knowing that each person is driven by different things. "I think the most effective leaders I've ever had are the ones who tried to figure out what makes each person tick," Malachowski says. "You need to be able to ask and understand what makes them happy. What is their priority? If you can do that, you can really get a good team." People will then work toward the mission, and when they work toward the mission, great things can be accomplished.

Mindful of her own accomplishments for the history of women in aviation, Malachowski knew she was indebted to those who served before her. "While a White House Fellow, I found myself in a unique situation to work on a project. I wanted to do something big." She chose to partner with the ongoing efforts of Wings Across America, an effort to document and recognize the history of the World War II women military pilots. Malachowski was able to bring the WASPs' story to the forefront on Capitol Hill. During the war, this select group of young women ferried planes around the United States for repair and maintenance and instructed male pilots who went into the war zones. They also served as test pilots. "These are women who enabled a lot of people like me to do what we do—fly military planes," Malachowski said. These women had to wait until 1977 to be granted veteran's status and were not nationally recognized for their trailblazing efforts and long-term impact on military women in aviation until awarded the Congressional Gold Medal in 2009 after the passing of Senate Bill 614. "This was a team effort, and I was the Washington, D.C., point man," Malachowski said. Vice Adm. Vivian Crea, the vice commandant and most senior-ranking aviator in the Coast Guard, was one of several military women whom Malachowski asked to help the effort. Crea was influential and involved and she even sent a letter of congratulations to each surviving WASP after they were awarded the Congressional Gold Medal.

Malachowski now looks forward to the next stage of her career. "I'm eager to get back into the cockpit," she said. "My heart wishes I was flying." She moved with her family to Seymour Johnson Air Force Base in North Carolina in 2010 and returned to flight status in the spring of 2011, flying the skies in the F-15E Strike Eagle. With two nineteen-month-olds and a husband deployed for seven months, on November 18, Malachowski assumed command of the 333rd Fighter Squadron leading two hundred airmen. The mission? To develop officers, train airmen, and grow warriors for F-15E Strike Eagle operations around the world.

3

From Sea to Shining Sea

Command Master Chief Mattie Wells, USN

*I've been pretty blessed being in the navy. I've had some good mentors
in my life to help me get to where I am today. I try to do the same
for my sailors by providing the tools for them to succeed.*

Command Master Chief Mattie M. Wells grew up in Monterey, a small Louisiana town about thirty miles west of the Mississippi River and nearly a four-hour drive northwest of New Orleans. The southern town, population of around a thousand people, was not a tourist destination, lacking a hotel or many restaurants to encourage visits. Encircled by bayous, the farmland of grassy plains and old oaks offered long, picturesque views of an untouched horizon that at the end of the day was filled with magnificent golden-pink Southern sunsets. The roads out of town were as winding as the great Mississippi, taking an hour or more to reach the interstate highway by driving alongside rice, soybean, and cotton fields and the occasional cow pasture. Wells's parents worked hard to provide for their fourteen children. Dad drove the school bus while Mom worked outside the home after the first eight of her children had grown up and moved away.

The school Wells and her siblings attended had roughly 450 students combined from grades K through 12. The Wells children, guided by a bright mom who believed they had a great future, decided that getting an education was the best way to land a job that would take them outside of Monterey to find success. Some of Wells's brothers and sisters did leave town and traveled the world by serving in the U.S. Marine Corps, Army, and Air Force. Mattie, the tenth child, graduated from high school in 1980 and went to college until she ran out of money and had to drop out. That's when she and a friend looked into the U.S. Air Force. Her test scores were lower than the air force required, but a recruiter who believed she had promise handed her application for the navy and Wells signed up with the U.S. Navy on May 3, 1983. "Here I am in the navy twenty-seven years later," Wells said at the time of the interview. "I just wanted to have a job and not have to live at home off my parents."

Wells, now forty-eight, rose to the highest enlisted rank possible and achieved something spectacular, selection as the commanding officer's enlisted adviser. She was a natural leader. Poised, well spoken, and steady in her resolve to do the best she could in her work, she inspired many men and women to emulate her example over the years. Wells was assigned back-to-back sea tours aboard three ships and was selected to serve as the key senior enlisted leader, command master chief (CMC).

In many ways, women who joined the navy in the early eighties, like Wells, fought battles of their own serving on board warships. They fought for equality and respect within the steel hulls of the U.S Navy's mightiest fighting fleet. Still novel to the historically male world of the seagoing services, women aboard ships were presumed by some men to bring bad luck upon the crew. Others treated the women as if their purpose was to serve the men.

Wells said of her accomplishments and longevity, "It was never something I intended to do, to be honest. . . . Beyond my initial enlistment my thought was to do my four years and get out." Her plan was to go back to Louisiana. She was used to living in a small town. Living away from home, and being in the navy, was a challenge. But Wells was mindful of her mother's guidance: *Work hard to the best of your ability in whatever you decide to do.* "That's all I ever did. That's all I ever do. Work hard to do the best job that I had regardless of what the situation was," Wells said. As she got promoted, her responsibilities increased, and her decision to leave faltered. "I think my calling was to stay in the navy," she said of her nearly three decades of service.

Modest about her success and overcoming challenges along the way, Command Master Chief Wells became a role model, a leader for both men and women, and a mentor for younger sailors. Starting out at the lowest enlisted rank, she completed boot camp, or basic training, in Orlando, Florida, in 1983 and continued on to Apprenticeship Training at the Naval Training Command also located there. Wells was then assigned her first tour afloat aboard a submarine tender, the USS *Emory S. Land* (AS-39) in Norfolk, Virginia. The ship did not go out to sea more than two or three days at a time and did most of its replenishment and repair work pierside.

"The guys were still in that mentality that women were here for their benefit," she said. "You had the stigma that if you were not sleeping around with the guys, you must be sleeping around with the women. To overcome that, I had to work harder than anybody else so that no one said a word about what I was doing in my personal life." Wells grew up in a very strict household in which her mother taught her right from wrong. "It wasn't that we'd get out of the house and hang out with the boys. We just didn't do stuff like that. I think that carried over with me in the navy. Plus, I wasn't a seventeen- or eighteen-year-old. When I came in I was twenty-one. I was a little more mature than some of these girls who came in right after high school." This negative perception of service women was not something she had been aware of when she agreed to serve, and it was not one that she validated.

It was during this assignment that Wells had a confrontation that forever changed the way she conducted herself at work. "It started with another individual, a 1st class petty officer, who had thirteen or fourteen years in the service," said Wells, who at the time was a less experienced, 3rd class petty officer with only two years in the navy. He accused her of being derelict in her duties because she logged in the receipt of a very important communications message and did not notify the duty officer that it was in house. The 1st class petty officer told her supervisors and commanding officer that Wells did not know what she was doing, although she had done everything she was supposed to do with the message except make that notification. The accusation initiated an investigation. Wells then had to go before the Commanding Officers Non-Judicial Punishment hearing about the investigation's findings, and the command held Wells accountable for not notifying the duty officer. "After that, I made sure that I took nothing for granted. I played by the rules and made sure that no one could say that I was not doing my job," says Wells. "That little event changed the way I conducted business." She was strictly professional, even while working side by side with a best friend.

While serving aboard the *Emory S. Land*, Wells was non-designated, which meant she did not have a job or career track. She thus had an opportunity to choose the rate or profession she wanted to pursue. The guidance of a female chief on board the ship helped Wells avoid succumbing to the pressures of serving and being a woman in the navy and helped her excel. "Some women had a hard time because they didn't know how to deal with it," said Wells. "I had somebody to focus on me, mentor me in the right career field." The chief reviewed Wells's record to see what she qualified for and made appropriate suggestions. One of them was becoming a radioman (RM), which is now called IT or information technology. This field appealed to her because it would mean working in the same closed-door environment in which she had been an apprentice. She enjoyed dealing with message traffic and classified materials while also being responsible to the command for critical, sensitive information they needed while on patrol. With that goal in mind, Wells had a direction but still planned to leave the navy in 1987, or after serving her four years.

Required to complete her commitment aboard ship, she talked with a navy career counselor before finishing the obligation in 1987. During the conversation the counselor asked what would keep her in the navy. "I said if I could get orders to Florida, I'd stay." Wells figured this request would go nowhere because everyone requests Florida. She was a junior enlisted petty officer "going through the motions" and just thinking about getting out. The counselor called one day and said, "I have orders for you to a communications center in Jacksonville, Florida."

"I was caught off guard because I did not expect him to take the time to find me orders to Jacksonville or any part of Florida. He upheld his end of the bargain so I upheld mine. That was it. I went on from there," said Wells. She had also gained a valuable insight that she used to guide her when she encountered chauvinism in the workplace: "Once they knew you were there to do your job and you did it just as well as the guys, they didn't bother you."

Jacksonville presented new opportunities that would take her around the world. Wells attended Radioman "C," an apprentice school to become a radioman, for two months in San Diego, California. After graduating Wells was a fully qualified radioman, which meant she was cleared to work in a classified room, behind a very secure combination-locked door, sending and receiving messages and communications for the commanding officer of a ship or land station. This earned her assignments at communications stations in Jacksonville, Florida from 1987 to 1989, as well as tours of duty in Diego Garcia and Puerto Rico (over the next few years), and with the Defense Information Systems Agency, helping with communications management control activities in Arlington, Virginia from 1994 to 1996.

By 1997, as an experienced petty officer and expert in her rate, she accepted orders for her next afloat tour aboard the USS *Chancellorsville*, a 567-foot guided-missile cruiser, home ported in Yokosuka, Japan, with a complement of more than 360 enlisted crew, 27 chiefs, and 33 officers. Wells was tasked with applying all her training and experience ashore to the front lines as an information technology specialist and leader aboard the ship. Their afloat missions included detecting, classifying, and tracking hundreds of potential targets simultaneously in the air, on the surface, and under the sea. The ship's arsenal could destroy targets using a variety of weapons, including ship- and helicopter-launched torpedoes, deck guns, surface-to-air and surface-to-surface missiles, rapid-fire close-in weapons, and electronic jammers and decoys. The ship deployed to the Persian Gulf April 6, 1999, with the USS *Kitty Hawk* battle group.

Following her tour aboard the USS *Chancellorsville*, Wells was selected to serve as a detailer at Navy Personnel Command in Millington, Tennessee in 2000. For the next three years, she reviewed enlisted records and the assignment requests of the service members and decided where to send them for their next tour of duty.

In 2003 she returned to Virginia for assignment aboard the USS *Bataan*, an 844-foot, 40,500-ton amphibious assault ship that could move in excess of twenty knots. The crew supported more than eighteen hundred marine troops, the equivalent of one Marine Expeditionary Unit, in operations for the Persian Gulf War, including Operation Enduring Freedom and Operation Iraqi Freedom from January to March of 2004. Their mission was to enable the navy and Marine Corps team to transition seamlessly from the sea to the land battle in order to help stabilize Iraq. "We had to take tanks and whatever else they needed and off-load it in Kuwait," said Wells. She served with more than a hundred officers and a thousand enlisted crew members aboard the Norfolk-based ship. She accompanied the ship and led the enlisted crew during these operational assignments to help with the war effort.

The USS *Bataan* was in port in Texas when Hurricane Katrina steamrolled into the Gulf of Mexico. "We were about to get underway and were told to stand fast until the hurricane passed," said Wells. Following the destruction caused by Hurricane Katrina, the crew was assigned to help with search, rescue, and relief efforts in Louisiana and assist with clean up and other volunteer work for the citizens of Mississippi.

Because of her leadership and excellence fulfilling her duties during her assignment aboard the USS *Bataan*, in 2005 Wells was promoted to the highest enlisted rank, master chief petty officer. Two years later, after completing the U.S. Navy Senior Enlisted Academy in Newport, Rhode Island, she earned her selection to the premier enlisted leadership post, command master chief.

"The reason I'm CMC today is because of Scott Kingsley, my old CMC aboard the USS *Bataan*," said Wells. "I guess he saw something in me I did not see in myself." At the time Wells was a senior chief with twenty years of service. Kingsley encouraged her to progress and select duties that would enable her to become a command master chief. He taught her about the roles and responsibilities of a command master chief, such as gauging morale and battle readiness and serving as the chief liaison between enlisted sailors and commissioned officers. He also involved Wells in the leadership discussions on board the USS *Bataan* about current issues affecting the crew, ranging from Disciplinary Review Boards for sailors who had violated the Uniform Code of Military Justice to career development boards for junior sailors needing guidance on job options and career paths. As the senior enlisted female, she would help with the conflicts that arose and needed to be explained to the commanding officer of the ship for the crew and, in particular, on behalf of the females. "They needed my input to make sure they were doing things in the right way for the women on the ship."

She credits Kingsley with providing opportunities for her to show she was probably a better leader than even she had given herself credit for. "I'm not a person that likes to be in the spotlight. All my life I was in communications, working behind a closed door requiring a combination to get in. People were not just stopping by," she said. "He took me from the background and put me in the fore light." Going there was not a comfortable transition for her. In fact, the first time she was asked to speak in front of the entire crew, as the emcee for an event, Wells almost refused to do it. "I was just scared to death. I almost made myself sick thinking, *How am I going to do this?*" Kingsley took her into his office and said, "Look, Senior Chief, it's actually my program and I want you to be the emcee." After that initial event, other people started asking her to do things in the spotlight even though she preferred to be in the background. The mentoring Kingsley provided Wells persists even though he has retired. They keep in touch, and Wells continues to seek his advice.

Wells was well prepared to serve as command master chief aboard the USS *Leyte Gulf* from 2007 to 2009. The guided-missile cruiser, equipped with Tomahawk cruise missiles, was named after the Philippine's Battle of Leyte Gulf, said to have been one of the greatest naval battles of World War II. They deployed to the Persian Gulf and for the ship's African Partnership mission. This was a training exercise with African nations as well as a counter-piracy operation off the Horn of Africa. Wells was amazed by how different the way of life was for the people of that country. "That's why I'll never change where I live," shared Wells about her American lifestyle. "It was an eye-opening experience. Things that we get and take for granted on a daily basis are so hard for people over there to acquire. Very humbling I should say."

Wells was appointed the command master chief for one of the navy's newest ships, the USS *Gravely* (DDG-107), in 2009. The guided-missile destroyer can operate independently and in conjunction with carrier strike groups, surface action groups, expeditionary strike groups, and replenishment groups.

In all her eleven years of sea duty, Wells only served simultaneously with five other female chiefs in the Chiefs' Mess, which can have over two dozen chiefs. The Chiefs' Mess is likened to the enlisted equivalent of the wardroom on a ship for officers. It is a room on the ship where the chiefs meet, eat their meals, and relax when off duty. Unless invited in, other members of the crew are restricted from using the room. The term also refers to the collective body of chiefs that serve as the enlisted leadership or board of directors who advise the commanding officer on issues and the needs of the enlisted crew. As the command master chief, Wells knew that it would be critical to have the backing of the chiefs to succeed, "because you can't do it by yourself," she shared. "The first thing you do after you take over the CMC job with the person you are relieving is to make sure everybody knows your expectations and that you are going to follow through."

Her biggest expectation of the Chiefs' Mess, and what she viewed as their first job, was to train the junior officers (JOs) who were coming into the navy right out of college or the Naval Academy. In training the JOs, the chiefs were training future leaders to become better naval officers. Her second expectation was that they develop their subordinates so that one day they would take the place of those in the mess. "JOs take the jobs of our commanding officers, and junior enlisted will one day become the chiefs," Wells explained.

Critical to the success of the JOs' training was to make sure they were listening, really listening, to the chiefs. Like Wells, the chiefs have experience serving in the military that they can share to benefit someone coming fresh out of college, even if it was a service academy. Chiefs, who commonly enlist right out of high school, do not typically have college degrees, and they work their way up the ranks. This disparity between junior officers and seasoned chiefs can create friction. As Wells often said to a JO, "Yes, you might have a degree, but experience-wise I've been in the navy probably longer than you've been alive. I know what it's going to take in order for you to succeed. So you might want to take the time to listen." Sometimes, she said, the officers who did not listen were allowed to fail at a task. "Then they realize that 'Oh, I've got go get on the same sheet of music as my chief.' When they come around there's an easy, good working relationship between the chief and junior officer."

In addition to various unit awards, Wells's personal awards include the Defense Meritorious Service Medal, the Joint Service Commendation Medal, the Navy Commendation Medal with two gold stars, and the Navy and Marine Corps Achievement Medal with four gold stars; each star represents a subsequent award. She was also a member of the All-Navy Women's basketball team four times throughout her career.

What has been the key to her success over the years? "It hasn't been a secret. This is what I tell all my sailors today: If you come to work and work hard, you're going to be fine, and that's all it takes—just a little discipline. Do your job when you're at work. Take care of yourself after work," said Wells. "I worked hard to do my best regardless of the situation. When anything needed to be done people said, 'We'll give it to Mattie because we know she's going to do it right.' You don't want to be that slacking person when everyone else is doing well."

Wells said that one of the things that kept her striving was the fact that she would hate to be kicked out of the navy for doing something stupid or for something that could have been avoided. "I never wanted to bring embarrassment or disappointment to my mother," she said. Her mother, Thelma Wells, who turned eighty-three in 2010, along with her father (who was eighty-six when he passed away in 1992), did the best they could do for their fourteen children. "We may not have had everything that we wanted, but we had everything we needed to survive," said Wells. "My parents did a great job."

Wells has not gotten married, does not have children, and has no regrets. "I have to be honest," she said. "I've been pretty blessed being in the navy. I've had some good mentors in my life, in the navy, to help me get to where I am today. That's why I try to do the same for my sailors in terms of providing the same tools for them to succeed."

4

Second Chance at Life

Lt. Col. L. Tammy Duckworth, USA
(Illinois National Guard)

I thought, Well, I don't know if I'm going to die today.
But I'm not going to die this minute.
I'm going to live through this minute.

It was seemingly a typical day in Iraq—dusty, getting hot. Flying the Black
Hawk helicopter, dropping people off and picking people up all over the country, was the order of the day for thirty-six-year-old Capt. L. Tammy Duckworth,
one of a handful of women to pilot a U.S. Army helicopter in Iraq. It was eight
months to the day since she had arrived in Iraq. During that day's flight, the
pilot in command, Chief Warrant Officer 4 Dan Milberg, a veteran pilot who
had flown in the Gulf War thirteen years earlier, accused her of being "on the
stick," the mechanism technically known as the cyclic used to fly the helicopter. Milberg teased that she was a "stick pig" for hogging the controls, something they both would alternate doing. While she flew the helicopter he would
answer the radio, check their course and direction, and instruct the crewmen
in the cabin of the helicopter. Milberg and Duckworth had flown together in
Iraq earlier in the deployment and got along well. Flying together again was
something they both enjoyed despite the stress of war. She understood his
sarcastic sense of humor and appreciated that he was always challenging her to
hone her skill as a pilot, even though she had already been recommended for
an Air Medal for her service in Iraq. Duckworth was serving as the battle captain and assistant operations officer for the five-hundred-soldier aviation task

force in Iraq. Before the sun set that evening, she would face an even greater challenge, made possible by the bravery of Milberg. She would have to choose between fighting for her life or losing it.

Duckworth was a child of a veteran of World War II and the Vietnam War. Her father rose from the enlisted ranks in the Marine Corps to become an army officer and married Duckworth's Thai mother. "I knew it was pure chance that my dad stayed and married my mom," Duckworth said, regarding her Amerasian ethnicity, given how many GIs did not. "Otherwise I would be one of those street kids selling whatever I could dig out of a garbage dump or [selling] myself." By the time Duckworth was a teenager her family moved from Southeast Asia, where she grew up in Thailand and Indonesia, to live in America. She saw the freedoms this country provided, unavailable to the Amerasian street children in Asia who lacked a home, nice clothes, and school. She realized how grateful she was to be an American. She saw young boys and girls on television in refugee camps overseas trying to prove their status as a child of a U.S. solider or of a citizen of the United States. "Immigration authorities would automatically accept your status as Amerasian, the child of an American GI, if you had freckles."

Being teased about her freckles was something that made a deep impression on her as a young girl in Southeast Asia. It was part of her understanding of how lucky she was and symbolic as to why the little girl, whose cultural traditions did not encourage females to volunteer for military service, did sign enlist. Her brother was expected to go into the service—and did serve in the Coast Guard for eight years. But, as Duckworth explained, the honor and integrity of military men and women appealed to her despite her culture's views. Based on her experiences both overseas and in the United States, she appreciates the "value system of serving this country and giving something back and being grateful for what we have. I felt that among the people that I served with in the military. They were not ashamed to be patriotic. They were not ashamed to talk about how much they loved this country. They were willing to sacrifice for it."

Sitting in the Black Hawk helicopter cabin behind Duckworth and Milberg was Spc. Kurt Hanneman, the gunner, and Sgt. Chris Fierce, the crew chief.

They were all in good spirits. The four were thankful that their mid-day mission had given them just enough time to stop in the Green Zone for lunch at the "fancy" chow hall. It was a rare treat. Made-to-order milkshakes and meals were on the menu. One of her favorites was stir-fried vegetables. Hanneman said he was interested in finding pewter Christmas ornaments. Finishing lunch and preparing to return to Balad, their base, for the evening, they scooped up a few of the ornaments with scenes of Babylon and other Biblical symbols, ideal to mail back to their families in the United States. It was November 12, 2004. They were betting they had just enough time for the packages to arrive home before the holidays. Duckworth also looked forward to returning to Balad because she was an avid swimmer, regularly swimming laps at the old Iraqi Officers' Club pool there.

The aircrew climbed in the helicopter and prepared for takeoff. There was a second helicopter, Chalk 2, flying in tandem on their route back to base. Duckworth knew their pilot, Chief Warrant Officer 4 Pat Meunks. She had flown with him before and knew he was a former medical evacuation, or medevac, pilot. Pilot-in-command Milberg, with the overall responsibility for the helicopter and crew safety, was a police officer in civilian life and an emergency medical technician, a skill that would prove fortunate for them very soon. The pilots were powering up the engines when they suddenly got a radio call from First Cavalry Division, the command in charge of operations for the region around Baghdad to the west and Sadr City, a suburb to the north. First Cavalry had requested they divert from their flight home to stop at Camp Taji, a military base, to pick up some passengers who needed to leave the base. The aircrew was tired; they had already worked a long day. Nevertheless, Duckworth convinced them to accept the mission, reasoning that it was the responsible thing to do. She felt especially so since it was during the Battle for Fallujah and thousands of U.S. and Iraqi troops were streaming into Fallujah in an all-out assault to drive insurgents out of the city. Ferrying passengers by air was a key way for people to get around. Milberg agreed.

By the time they arrived in Taji only one passenger needed a lift. The rest were gone. The passenger got aboard Chalk 2, and both aircraft lifted off for Balad. "We were just ten feet above the trees, just cruising along in a normal flight profile, probably one hundred knots," Duckworth remembered. "We were headed home."

She said to Milberg, "You know, you fly. It will give me a break and let me man the mission . . . a chance to be pilot in command." She had just given him the controls when their aircraft flew into an ambush. Duckworth heard the sound of death coming—TAP! TAP! TAP!—metal on metal. "I knew we'd been hit," Duckworth said. She turned towards Milberg shouting, "We've been f——ing hit!" Then she reached forward instinctively to hit the Global Positioning System (GPS) device in an attempt to lock down the coordinates of their attack. She was not sure if her fingers reached the GPS in time.

BOOM!

A blast of fire exploded outside her open cabin door. It snaked up through the floor of the cockpit, over her legs and right arm. It blew sections of her lower extremities off as it spread and took the back of her right arm as it advanced toward Sgt. Fierce.

Unaware of her own injuries, Duckworth focused on getting the aircraft carrying her buddies safely on the ground. She shouted again into the internal communications system that they'd been hit. No one responded, not even Milberg.

In fact, no one heard her. The avionics equipment had been blown out by the blast, severing any option of talking to one another over the main system. Duckworth thought she was the only one who was all right.

In Chalk 2, Pat Meunks witnessed the rocket-propelled grenade colliding with and tearing through his colleagues' helicopter. He immediately issued Mayday calls and asked for a medevac helicopter. From his experience as a medevac pilot he knew the aircrew would require skilled life-saving experts, and soon.

Only a few heartbeats had passed since the hit. Duckworth focused her last precious conscious moments on directing the cyclic in her right hand to command the helicopter's airborne direction and using her left hand to lower the collective—a flight control to alter the helicopter's ascent or descent—to decrease the helicopter's lift and rapidly rest the 18,000-pound machine gently on the ground, but the cyclic control was not responding. The complex system of hydraulics and linkages that gave her left hand control of the rotors above her head had failed. She was also extremely frustrated that the pedals were not responding. By pushing on the pedals with her right foot, the tail would shift right and the front of the helicopter should have turned to the left.

She would later discover that at that moment, neither the pedals nor the lower half of her legs were there anymore. She used all her will and body to try and keep flying: "How many times throughout the day do you look down to check that your feet are still there? You can feel them, so they're there. Well, I could feel them but they weren't there. I was really frustrated. I was like, *Great, the pedals aren't working. I hope Dan's got the pedals.*"

Enemy fire continued to strike unrelentingly. The helicopter filled with smoke. It was shaky, struggling to fly like a bird with a broken wing. Duckworth heard the pitch change on the number 2 engine. She was certain that it had sucked up a lot of foreign objects, shrapnel, and metal during the attack and explosion. She feared the worst. The engine would fail. They could spiral out of control, crash, and burn. "I was afraid we were going to go into the trees." She felt the intensity of the few seconds they had left in flight: "I have a terrible vocabulary when I'm in my uniform and in my aircraft. I was cussing to myself and thinking, *Where am I going to put this thing?* When, wow, in the middle of this palm grove was this grassy opening. It should not have been there, but it was. It was like God put it there. I was thinking, *This aircraft is going down here.* I didn't know I had slumped forward. I remember thinking that the gauges looked bigger than normal. It turned out that my face was about three inches from the gauges. I was trying to fly in that position."

The gauges had gone dark, dead. The pilots had no indication of their airspeed, altitude, or angles of flight. No alarms were going off. In the seconds that followed in slow motion she didn't realize that Milberg was also on the controls. "I felt the aircraft start to sink. I thought, *Oh no, the aircraft is going to lose power.* I tried to put the aircraft into an auto rotation."

Milberg, per protocol, took control of the helicopter and had begun what Duckworth planned, an approach for an emergency landing. He saw the opening between the palm trees and guided the aircraft toward it. Both pilots worked together to execute the precision maneuvers they had been trained to do to get the machine down on the ground without further destruction. Duckworth had her left hand on the collective. She thought her right was controlling the cyclic.

"One of the last things I remember was becoming indignant because there was grass coming through my chin bubble," said Duckworth. "I remember thinking, *Well, now, I didn't land this aircraft that hard.*" Normally the aircraft would sit at least four feet above the ground. The grass in that patchy area was about six feet tall, which explained why it was up and through the broken floorboards. They had completed a safe, soft landing, a point of great pride for pilots, especially these air assault pilots, to "kiss the ground" when landing so that their passengers don't feel a bump.

Still focused on procedure, she thought of what had to be done next to prevent a fire: *I've got to shut off the engines.* But as her hand reached up a few inches toward the controls, Duckworth blacked out.

Meunks landed his helicopter in front of the crippled one. Two of his crew members jumped out to help Milberg carry the injured over and get them safely inside before the insurgents advanced to close range. Hanneman had taken a shot in his tailbone. Fierce had severe injuries to one of his legs. They struggled in the uneven ground and tall grass, falling a few times. Milberg feared that insurgents would appear at any moment. They seemed very close at hand, judging by the sound of their firing weapons. Even though he thought Duckworth was dead, he ran back to get her body. As he carefully removed her from the pilot's seat, he noticed her right leg was missing. Then he saw it lying on the floor of the aircraft—about four inches of her right leg was sticking out of her combat boot, the rest was "just hamburger." Her left leg was nearly severed also but hanging by some tissue and skin. The blast had blown off the entire back side of her right arm.

Two U.S. aircraft, which had been flying a short distance behind Meunks and Milberg before the attack, flew circles overhead and provided a screen of bullet fire for cover to help keep the enemy away. They took several rounds from the enemy machine guns into the belly of their aircraft during the defensive maneuvers.

Meunks was airborne again, this time with the injured crew aboard. He tipped the nose down for forward flight and flew the helicopter as fast as it could go, back to Taji. Hanneman, Duckworth, and Fierce were transferred to the medical evacuation helicopter, waiting with rotors spinning, for the short flight to the Combat Surgical Hospital in Baghdad. It was Fierce who first noticed that Duckworth might still be alive. During the flight to Baghdad her body was lying on the floor near him. He noticed that warm blood was flowing onto the deck of the helicopter, but it was not his. Her heart was still beating! He alerted the medics. Initially reported killed in action, she had not received a tourniquet or any medical treatment. With this news, Fierce refused treatment for himself, insisting the medics take care of Duckworth first. She still had a chance.

From time of impact until the medevac helicopter landed in Baghdad, it had been no more than thirty minutes, but the medics did wonders stabilizing Duckworth during the flight. By the time they were going through the doors of the emergency room, she was awake and talking.

Ten days later Duckworth woke up at Walter Reed Army Medical Center, only five miles up the road from the White House. Stabilized by American medical teams in Iraq, she was evacuated for additional surgeries and a lengthy recovery at Walter Reed. Going in and out of consciousness, she knew the journey to recovery would test her courage and endurance at an entirely new level. This was a matter of life and death, and she had a lot of questions: Could she live through the relentless pain? Was her life worth living as a triple amputee? Did she deserve to live if she lost the helicopter?

Over fifteen months some of the events following the crash-landing came together in her mind like little puzzle pieces. Bits of her memory were lost entirely because of the traumatic experience. Some parts of her life were only reconnected when eyewitnesses told the story to her.

One of these was the fateful day she met Sgt. 1st Class Childs, who had been the noncommissioned officer in charge of the emergency room in Baghdad the day Duckworth and her crew were brought in by the medevac helicopter. Childs had since been reassigned to Walter Reed, where their paths crossed one afternoon. "I was rolling along outside in my wheelchair. He walked by me, did a double take, and said, 'I know you! You came to my emergency room. We had a conversation.' I said, 'I don't remember.' He said, 'Let me tell you. . . .'"

When the aircrew was rolled into the emergency room in Baghdad, Childs told Duckworth that he had noticed that parts of both of her lower legs and her right arm were destroyed or missing entirely. Yet, she was awake and talking to the doctors and nurses. "It is known that if you have one femoral artery cut, you should bleed to death in four and one-half minutes," said Duckworth. The heat from the explosion had cauterized her leg wounds. "I lasted at least thirty minutes with all the arteries in my left leg and all the arteries in my right leg and right arm cut. I was incredibly lucky. I had some great people taking care of me and probably a little divine help too."

Childs knew that the aircrew's gunner, Hanneman, had taken a round to his tailbone. The crew chief, Fierce, almost lost his leg. The blast that exploded mostly on Duckworth also injured him gravely because he had been sitting right behind her in its fiery path. Skilled U.S. military doctors and nurses were able to save his leg and Fierce would later return to flight status. Duckworth was not as lucky.

Childs said to Duckworth, "The three of you were the most obnoxious. You were propped up on the one limb that you had left. You wouldn't shut up, kept asking, 'How is my crew? How are my men? Check on my crew,'" Childs recalled. "You wouldn't answer any of our questions about how you were doing." Childs told her that the crew chief was also asking a barrage of questions and repeatedly asking, "How's Capt. Duckworth?" Hanneman was walking around refusing medical treatment saying, "Take care of Capt. Duckworth first." The three of them, though not close friends, had bonded from serving together in Iraq. "That kicks in," said Duckworth. "You're buddies."

Childs joked that the medical team finally put all of them under to quiet them so they could work on their injuries.

Hearing this story was one of the things she was most proud of about the day her life changed. "I wasn't crying and thinking of myself," she admitted. "Even then, coming in through those doors I was thinking about my crew. That's important to me. But it wasn't anything unique for an American soldier."

What Duckworth endured during her recovery was exceptional, and though she would have willingly died for her country, she hadn't expected to suffer grave injuries while serving on active duty. For nine days she struggled to stabilize enough to undergo additional surgery at Walter Reed. She was unconscious. Her husband, Maj. Bryan Bowlsbey, an army officer in the Illinois National Guard, joined her, standing a bedside vigil with other members of her family. He had been saying the same three things over and over again, a mantra, in hopes that she would hear him and be comforted knowing that she was receiving the best medical care:

You were injured. You are safe. You're at Walter Reed.
You were injured. You are safe. You're at Walter Reed.

Waking up was a slow, sluggish process. She knew she had been injured. She knew she was safe. She knew she was at Walter Reed. The message had been received.

A half day or more before she was fully awake, even though the tube had been removed from her mouth, she could not tell anyone around her she heard them talking. She was aware that her beloved husband was in the room talking to the nurse about her recovery and the necessity for regular deep breathing exercises to help her regain her lung strength. His back was toward her. The nurse, observing that Tammy's eyes were open, gently turned him around. Bryan leaned over toward her and said, "I love you, honey. How are you?"

She looked up into his eyes. "I think my first words were 'I love you. Put me to work.' I had heard him talking with [the nurse] about how much therapy I was going to have to do." She was ready to work, to survive. First, she asked for some pain medication. "My legs hurt. Please ask the doctor for some pain medication for my legs." Bryan had to find the nearest resident to help break the news. She no longer had her full legs. She said, "Okay," then told Bryan to go take a shower because he smelled so bad. He didn't want to go, but she insisted. Her sense of smell was hypersensitive from all the medications her body had been given, and she was quickly becoming nauseated. "I told him, 'Honey, you need to go take a shower.' He said that's when he knew that I was back and I was okay." His greatest fear was not that she had lost her legs but that she would have some sort of brain injury and would no longer be the woman he loved. Now he knew she was okay. Everything was going to be fine.

"I don't know what day I woke up. I know that they could not operate on me until Monday," recalled Duckworth. "They were going to do this major operation, put in epidural and pain blocks to cut off the flow of information from the lower half of my body and my right arm." She longed for Monday. It was five days away. During those days she could not sleep. She could not move. She had no energy. "All I could think about was the excruciating pain. I felt like my legs were on fire and being skinned at the same time. It felt like somebody was sitting there slicing off the skin in strips, at the same time somebody was pouring molten lead on my legs," she gravely confessed. "That's what it felt like. And I couldn't move any part of my body." The doctors kept her sedated. They did not want her to be fully aware. "There was no reason to bring me out so I could feel the pain."

Even so, the morphine they had prescribed did not work. It did nothing for the pain, but instead it made her hallucinate and vomit. The doctor told her husband that it was like she had never taken drugs before, calling her "narcotics naïve." In fact, they had not seen anyone with this condition before. Duckworth had never taken drugs nor did she drink alcohol because she did not tolerate it very well. "I know it's crazy for a pilot to not drink, but my body had a very low tolerance to any type of narcotics, and it just rejected them," she revealed. It took about five days, or 120 hours, to wean the morphine from her system and figure out what to do to help her cope. She wondered if she could really wait for that time to pass.

Many family members helped her through the agonizing seconds of every painful minute. "My mom, poor thing, sat next to my bed and kept trying to stoke my arm or touch any skin that was available, trying to caress me to be comforting." Duckworth said. "It hurt so much anytime anyone even touched the sheets on my bed. I didn't even have the strength in me to tell my mom to please stop because she was hurting me." It took an entire day to save up her strength. She looked at her mom and said, "'Mom, it hurts, stop.' She left the room crying because she had been hurting me. I wanted to say, 'No, no, you're fine,' but I didn't have the strength."

Hanging opposite her bed was one of those institutional, round black-and-white clocks frequently found in government offices. "I could see it. I remember thinking, *I'm not going to live through this. I cannot live through this. I'm going to die.* Then I looked at that clock and watched the second hand tick. I thought, *Well, I don't know if I'm going to die today. But I'm not going to die this minute. I'm going to live through this minute.* So, I started counting down the minutes with each second, then started over again." Talking to herself, whispering—it felt good to be doing something, taking control. "Your brain does strange things when you're medicated, delusional." Fluent in Thai and Indonesian, she broke up the monotony a bit by switching languages before returning to English. Her mother counted with her in Thai. Her brother counted with her in English.

One day, 1st Sgt. Juanita Wilson showed up in Duckworth's hospital room. Wilson had lost one of her arms just three months earlier. Duckworth was the fifth woman amputee from the Iraq conflict. "She was the first person that looked at me and said, 'I know it hurts. It will stop.' She took off her artificial arm so I could see the stump," Duckworth recalled. Wilson revealed in that moment her weakness, her vulnerability, and her strength. "She asked, 'Can I stand here next to you?' I think I nodded, yes." For four or five days, Wilson stood next to Duckworth's bed and helped her count from zero to sixty for hours at a time. Duckworth would get delusional, turn away. When she looked back, Wilson was still there. Her presence was comforting. Wilson understood her pain. Her fear. Her doubt.

"She was this kind of oasis of serenity and strength," Duckworth said, and she began to cry. "I'm sorry. I get emotional when I think about this. I later asked Bryan, 'Was she really there?'" She knew that if Wilson went through it she, too, could survive. "There were like these invisible strands of strength and serenity coming from her. I clung to that. At one point, I looked at my husband and said, 'I have to go now.' He thought I meant I have to die now. I had said, 'I'm sorry, I have to circle the wagons.' What I meant was I had no energy to interact with any of you. I had to shut down to my very core to deal with this pain. I had nothing left. I think I went into myself, I don't know for how long. I came back just in time to be operated on. That scared him. He thought I was going to die. It was unbelievable pain."

Monday finally arrived and Duckworth was going into surgery. The doctors were going to put in a pain block. "There was nothing left in me, no strength, when they finally took me in."

On her way into the operating room she noticed a familiar name on the operating board schedule above hers. CHRIS FIERCE. She asked, "Is Sgt. Fierce here?" She was told he was going to have surgery at the same time. "That's my crew chief," she replied. "The nurses were very kind. Even though they weren't supposed to, they pushed our gurneys together so they touched. We could talk. We just cried like babies. I apologized to him for getting him hurt and for crashing the aircraft."

Duckworth had been devastated since she regained consciousness, believing that she deserved to lose her legs because she thought she had hurt her crew and crashed the aircraft: "I had obviously not done a good job as a pilot. All you've got to do as a pilot is land the damn thing, and yet I had let my crew and my buddies down." Even just days before the operation her husband knew she was crying from guilt. He brought her a picture of the aircraft sitting in the field where they landed it to prove that she was wrong, that she had landed the helicopter safely, against all odds. She did not believe him, convinced that the men who trusted her with their lives had been let down. She felt she had failed as an officer, as a soldier.

As she was making her tearful apology in the operating room, Fierce corrected her, "No, you guys landed it." Now she was relieved. She believed him. It must be true, "and that's why I've been okay ever since. I don't need to be the hero. I don't need to be the one that carried everybody to safety," she shared. "I just needed to know that I did everything until my last breath to do my job." She was at peace with her wounds. She earned them and was not to be pitied. The Soldier's Creed—the army's oath each soldier must take based on the ideals of loyalty, duty, respect, and selfless service—was critical to her survival. She posted the creed outside her hospital room so that people coming in to visit her knew by its words that a soldier was within, one who placed the mission first, did not give up, did not accept defeat or leave a fallen comrade. She also put it on the wall opposite her bed so she could read it every day. On tough days the words carried her though and helped her achieve little victories.

Chief Warrant Officer 4 Dan Milberg was Duckworth's hero. He also lived by the creed. With the enemy attacking from just two hundred meters away, Milberg had risked his life to save the lives of the aircrew by pulling them off the helicopter and helping them to Meunks's waiting aircraft. "Dan thought I was dead. After he landed that aircraft and got everybody over to Chalk 2, he should have taken off with them," Duckworth said. "But he came back and carried me out. I think every day about him doing that. I go on. I try to live up to him coming back and carrying me out." Milberg received a Distinguished Flying Cross for his heroism.

Sgt. Chris Fierce knew the engine needed to be shut off after they crash-landed. He unbuckled and, with his leg hanging and almost completely severed by the explosion, crawled forward through the wreckage and burning metal to secure the engine.

Spc. Kurt Hanneman, even with a bullet lodged in his tailbone from enemy fire, took the .60-caliber machine gun and created a defense against the nearby attackers. He did his best to maintain security to the rear of the downed helicopter.

"It's about the crew," said Duckworth, who received a Purple Heart. "People try to make me more than I am. And I'm not."

Lt. Col. L. Tammy Duckworth has dedicated her life to public service and has became a political figure advocating for disability rights and veterans. She ran for a U.S. congressional seat in the Sixth District of Illinois, losing to her Republican opponent by only 2 percent of the vote. During Senator Barack Obama's successful run for the presidency, she was an electoral college delegate. As a champion of veterans' needs, she was appointed director of the Illinois Department of Veterans' Affairs on November 21, 2006, and until 2008 she took care of providing for Illinois's veterans by creating and funding new programs. She supervised several veteran assistance programs, roughly more than $70 million worth. Nationally a strong voice for veterans' rights and the need for increased veteran benefits, she testified before both the U.S. House and Senate, striving to make sure those who have served in the military are not forgotten. She has testified before the Senate Committee on Veterans Affairs numerous times about what needs to be done to help veterans.

President Obama nominated her, and the Senate confirmed the appointment on April 22, 2009, to serve as the Department of Veterans Affairs (VA) assistant secretary for public and intergovernmental affairs. Duckworth advised the secretary of veteran affairs on matters relating to media and public affairs and oversaw programs relating to homeless veterans, consumer affairs, and the department's six national rehabilitative special event programs.

Promoted to lieutenant colonel in the Illinois Army National Guard, she retained her commission and retrained to pilot aircraft in the civilian world. As she admits, "I miss being what I used to be, which was an army helicopter pilot. I'm not that anymore. I tried really, really hard to fly the Blackhawk again." She flew in the simulator, but the artificial limbs lack the technology to help her operate the pedals with her feet. Yet, she's happy with her life now. "Could I have really whined and not taken the detour to Taji? Sure! But I won't change my service in Iraq. I'm proud of it. I'm proud of the guys I served with. Yeah, I wish every day that I had my legs, but they're gone. I can't dishonor Dan and all those guys who fought so hard to keep me alive by sitting at home and feeling sorry for myself. Plus," she laughed, "they'd come over to my house and kick my ass for feeling sorry for myself and give me a real hard time. So, you just go on."

Soldier's Creed

I am an American Soldier.

I am a warrior and a member of a team.

I serve the people of the United States, and live the Army Values.

I will always place the mission first.

I will never accept defeat.

I will never quit.

I will never leave a fallen comrade.

I am disciplined, physically and mentally tough, trained and proficient in my warrior tasks and drills.

I always maintain my arms, my equipment and myself.

I am an expert and I am a professional.

I stand ready to deploy, engage, and destroy, the enemies of the United States of America in close combat.

I am a guardian of freedom and the American way of life.

I am an American Soldier.

www.army.mil/values

5

"The Few, the Proud, the Women Marines"

1st Sgt. Brenda R. Chrismer, 1st Sgt. Debra A. Sharkey (Ret.),
and Capt. Catherine D. Florenz Michaud, USMC

*While the establishment cannot change the tendency of some men
to assume the inferiority of women, I have never seen or experienced
a denial of opportunity to any female Marine. We fight for recognition,
respect, and honor, side by side with male Marines, and only the best—
male or female—survive. I think it is important to note that
I do not think of myself as a female Marine. I am a Marine.*

—Capt. Catherine Florenz Michaud

By the sound of it, the enemy's mortar rounds were getting closer and closer. Praying was not going to stop their advance toward Staff Sgt. Brenda R. Chrismer of the U.S. Marine Corps. She was trapped by the enemy's incoming rounds in a crude trailer used as a camp shower. Just outside, spiraling dirt was shaken free from the dry Iraqi desert floor by the powerful explosions. The loudness of the advancing insurgent attacks increased not only her fear but also the life-threatening moment's intensity to a deafening pitch.

Just moments before it was a quiet, sunny, and extremely hot afternoon at the Forward Operating Base Kalsu near Iskandariya, Iraq, approximately twenty miles south of Baghdad. Surrounded by Shiites and Sunnis, the area was known as the "triangle of death." Chrismer and a team of twenty-six enlisted artillerymen were the only detachment of U.S. Marines assigned to this facility in 2005. The others were quite a bit younger and less experienced in detainment duties than Chrismer, who had specialized in prisoner management. She taught the men, who were nineteen to twenty-five years old, how to manage enemy detainees held at Kalsu, one of five internment facilities in Iraq. If deemed necessary, the prisoners would be transported from the temporary holding facility to the Abu Ghraib prison for extensive questioning and confinement. Infamous photographs distributed by worldwide news outlets and the Internet had made Abu Ghraib's name synonymous with torture in 2004. After the Abu Ghraib story broke, the marines were brought in to help with the handling and detention of Iraqi prisoners of war and to prevent more abuse.

Their job was particularly edgy and wearing. Sometimes they'd stay inside the detention facilities. Or, usually in the morning, they'd go out of the "wire," or protected area, on convoys to transfer the Iraqi prisoners from the temporary holding facility to Abu Ghraib. Then they'd return to the detention center using the main supply routes or roadway, all the while under protective escort by army National Guard soldiers from New Orleans, Louisiana, many of whom had lost their homes when Hurricane Katrina devastated their neighborhoods.

The marines worked twelve-hour shifts everyday, supervising anywhere from eighty-five to a hundred prisoners of war. Chrismer and her peer, Gunnery Sgt. Carlos R. Quiroz, worked back-to-back shifts as joint advisers. "We'd process the detainees, and do the fingerprinting and paperwork to get them into the system," Chrismer said. "It was hard for [the marines]. They had the grunt (infantry) mentality. They needed to learn that our mission there was important, and that we couldn't be sky-lined or sidetracked by all the negative publicity that was spiraling out of control due to the army personnel and their methods of handling detainees." She said the marines treated the detainees humanely, regardless of how they acted or the things they said to the soldiers. Even when the detainees prayed for ill will to come to the marines, the marines dealt with them respectfully.

Chrismer had specifically deployed to Iraq for Iraqi Detention Operations as a corrections adviser for enemy detentions. She knew the job well and was strong mentally and tough physically. Over the past thirteen years she had worked in military brigs in Japan; Camp Pendleton, California; and Parris Island, South Carolina. While serving in San Diego, she was assigned to the Marine Corps Absentee Collection Unit as a cross-country chaser and apprehension staff noncommissioned officer in charge. For other assignments she served as a marine combat training instructor and basic warrior training instructor, teaching courses of instruction to both male and female recruits. These classes included the use of field telephones, digging fighting holes, and even setting up fields of fire in the area to the left and right of an individual's fighting position for which they are responsible. Being the only female marine on the team in Iraq did not dissuade her. At thirty-three years old, it was natural for her to work in a mostly male military environment. In doing so, over time, she became less feminine-looking. "My appearance has gone this way because I am in the Marine Corps. I'll compete with the best of them. I have to fit in anyway I can," she said. "I am in a man's world." Her black hair was cropped short; her manner was professional, militant. No makeup. No lipstick. "Service before self" had become her coat of armor and the corps her life. Ordered into this war zone, responsible for two dozen young men, she skillfully trained and led her combat-tested team to success in detention operations without hesitation.

Three to five times a week the camp received enemy fire. Their chow hall and Internet phone center, which was basically a tent, were blown up. Despite the fear the young men felt for themselves during these attacks, which also targeted the prison, the job of the U.S. Marine Corps detachment was to make sure each detainee was secure and fed three meals a day. Round the clock, they checked up on them, looking through little side windows to make sure the detainees were not trying to kill themselves. Constantly upgrading both facilities for more protection and security, the marines also assisted in the construction of better housing for the detainees—who were also given a prayer mat, water, and a sleeping mat. "Typically the detainees were held in this small facility for a period of no more than two weeks," said Chrismer. "Interrogation teams talked to them and those that needed further questioning or investigation went to Abu Ghraib. The rest were released back to their community."

At night the forward operating base was ordered "lights out." The main supply route was a little higher than their tents and any light would attract attention to their dwellings, making them a target of an enemy attack. "You sit around at night in the detention facility. They [the marines on duty] are fighting the sleep monster with no lights on in the camp," said Chrismer. "The job itself is redundant and boring. For the most part it's like babysitting." When patrolling the detention center, they used "moonbeams" (flashlights) to check up on the occupants. "We'd walk around the camp. Iraq is pitch-black dark, especially with no moonlight," said Chrismer. "It's tough. Kind of scary."

Off watch, sometimes, the marines could sit and talk and she helped them deal with being far from home, missing family and friends. "The long distance and time away can bring you down. Missing a first child being born, wives upset with them because they're not there," recalled Chrismer. "I think they can relate to having a female to just listen to them. I gave them advice because they would always beat themselves up emotionally about not being there for their families. I never judged them when they cried, never told anyone. It didn't make them less of a marine. That was our thing."

More than a confidante and leader, Chrismer was responsible for their safety. She had great praise for the team of young men, lance corporals and corporals, the lowest of the noncommission ranks. Some had previous combat experience. The novelty of this assignment required the enlisted to learn how to deal with the pandemonium created when the prison came under shelling by insurgents. Chrismer explained, "When we received the incoming, my marines were tough. They didn't leave their post unprotected. Wooden hatches had to be closed up, to ensure each detainee was secured, even as the detainees were chanting 'praise Allah.' It's nerve-racking when you hear each mortar round coming in a little bit closer. The ground shakes. You pray it's the last one. They're scared and young, but they never let it faze them."

Chrismer knew that their nerves were a mess after the "all clear" was given following the attacks. Everyone was trying to maintain composure. She led them to immediately get accountability. She ran to find out if her marines were okay without showing her own fear, knowing that sometimes detainees and marines were in a large overflow tent with wooden floors where shrapnel ripped through.

There was nothing unusual about Chrismer's decision to take a bottled water shower in the new trailer on an intensely hot, sunny day. The trailer was a welcome addition to the sparse camp. Forward Operating Base Kalsu rarely had running water because the generators never worked. It was too hot. By mid-day, temperatures climbed to 120 degrees Fahrenheit. Wearing flak jackets with built-in bulletproof plates and other heat-confining uniform gear like helmets caused their body temperatures to rise. Their weaponry and equipment amounted to about sixty pounds that a soldier was responsible to maintain. The combination of heavy, heat-trapping gear and the intense heat made everyone sweat profusely. The sweat, mixed with the roughness of the gear on tender, raw skin, created prickly heat rashes across backs and necks. A shower, even with bottled water, offered a bit of temporary relief from the discomfort. It was as close to a spa as anyone could get in the desert. Naturally, when the time seemed right, Chrismer decided to seek a few moments of reprieve and indulge in this rare luxury. She had just soaped up when she heard it: BOOM! BOOM!

"I'm thinking, *No this can't be happening*," said Chrismer. Her only way to survive the blasts was to get out of there and dash to the bunker for safety. Her mind raced. Her feet slipped and slid on the wet, soapy deck. She tried to escape through the door, but bottles of water were now on the floor rolling all around her. She nearly fell. Chrismer grabbed for a towel to wipe a little of the dripping shampoo from her face. Her eyes burned. She squinted trying to see a way out.

BOOM!

This one was louder, closer.

BOOM!

The frail trailer shook as the mortar exploded nearby. Chrismer would normally be working in the detention center or giving orders and providing direction to keep the men safe and the detainees secure. She would also be running from bunker to bunker, checking up on the whereabouts and safety of her fellow marines during an attack. The accountability was procedural. But now this leader was alone.

Common sense told her to run. She grabbed her physical fitness shorts, shirt, and towel and sprinted for the bunker just outside the trailer door. Flying down the three steps, she threw herself to the ground to escape the incoming barrage of fire. She remembered hearing the haunting squeak of the trailer's hatch flying back and forth in the wind. "I was just sitting there holding my clothes. I couldn't put them on because I was terrified," she confessed. "I left behind my skivvies, kind of not important. I knew I should get dressed but just could not imagine that this would happen to me. It was just my kind of luck." Crouched inside the bunker she watched the ground quaking intensify as the powerful rounds closed in. "Rocks, dirt, shrapnel. I just sat there. Soapy. Naked. Unintentional tears turned into dirt tears. A couple of my marines came looking for me. They knew I had just gotten off shift." As she had done for each of them many times before, they now ran bunker to bunker searching for her.

She survived this near-death experience only to live through a shrapnel hit yet again when her body-armored vest took a shrapnel hit later. Sadly, she would bear witness to others who were not as lucky. Once she approached a U.S. Army soldier minutes after a land mine exploded under the front driver's side tire of his vehicle. She could see that he had lost his legs, but he fought desperately for his life as he was medevaced from the site.

Chrismer gained a greater appreciation for the small things in her life as an outcome of these experiences in Iraq, things often taken for granted because they were always there, like her family.

Growing up with seven siblings in Edinburg, Texas, she was a daughter in a traditional Mexican family. Like her mother, Chrismer was smart and a great athlete. Her childhood home still contains dozens of first place trophies she earned in races. At the age of nine, Chrismer was running 5Ks and 10Ks against seventeen-year-old racers and was setting new records. By the time she was twelve, Chrismer had completed two half marathons. Her parents were very proud of her all-around athletic skill in basketball, volleyball, cross-country, and track.

Unlike her mother, Chrismer did not feel her place was to be at home cooking and cleaning. Right after high school she enlisted in the Marine Corps. "Primarily because I was running away from growing up," she recalled. "I had a tough time with my childhood." When she was fifteen, doctors told Chrismer that her mother, who suffered from heart disease and diabetes, had only another year to live. "Any illness you could imagine, she had it," Chrismer said. What she admired most about her mother was that she was tough mentally and physically. Her weak health did not get her down. In fact, her mom lived another twenty years.

Chrismer's father had served in the Marine Corps for four years and then worked various jobs in Texas. Tragically, he broke his back in a vehicle accident when Chrismer was ten years old. Family and friends helped them manage while their father was recovering in a full body cast. "I think that was one of the things that made me want to be a Marine even more," Chrismer said. "He was strong, tough, and very persistent. He had metal rods in his back, but he got past that and was walking again like he never broke his back in three places. I think I get my stubbornness from him."

Childhood for Chrismer was difficult and something she will not discuss in detail. "I think everyone always wants a better life. I honor my parents. They did the best that they could," she admitted. "You see it now as you grow up. I think I saw it most when I got back from Iraq. It was simpler then to learn the appreciation of things and realize that there is so much that's insignificant. Really! Because I had to watch my marines day-by-day, wondering if they would have to fight for their lives. Suddenly the hurtful family arguments and drama were insignificant: siblings fighting, phone calls not returned, the everyday bickering. It just did not matter."

Because she made a good salary as a marine, Chrismer used to get stressed out and worked up because she felt a financial responsibility to help her siblings. "I couldn't give them enough money to support them in time of need. If I could, I would give them all my paychecks." In time, she realized that it was not her sole responsibility to bail them out of every problem. At some point they needed to rely on themselves.

Being in Iraq was life changing for Chrismer, "as it was for almost everyone." In turn, her leadership and dedication to service before self was transformative for the marines she worked with. "The Marine Corps is a family. We watch each other's back. We value that. We value life, American life."

Following her tour in Iraq, she became a drill instructor. In April of 2006, she reported to Oscar Company, Fourth Recruit Training Battalion, located at Parris Island, South Carolina—the only place where female marines go through recruit training for the Corps. After completing two cycles of seventy training days each as a drill instructor, she advanced to senior drill instructor for two more cycles and then rose to series gunnery sergeant for a total of eight cycles.

Chrismer noticed that the women under her instruction, joining the Corps in the mid-2000s, are much more educated and mature than women were when she enlisted in 1992. The young women of today want skills, she explained. The recruiters encouraged them to enlist by promoting the benefits the service offers. Recruits can become marksmen, skilled in martial arts with battlefield training, and the Corps will instill discipline, spirit, honor, courage, and commitment. "The intelligence level of the women recruits today is so high. We refer to them as the millennium group. I think my generation was the Pepsi generation," Chrismer laughed. "All I wanted to do was join the Corps and run off to the Gulf War. I was too late for that. I was so naïve about the military. I was excited when we (women) were issued boots too," she said. Importantly, many more jobs are now inclusive for women, who are no longer limited to administrative positions.

Twenty, ten, even five years ago, the Marine Corps was a very different place for women. Their acceptance, job opportunities, and physical standards were restricted compared to the men's. They were negatively stereotyped simply because they were female.

In the early nineties, when Chrismer reported for duty, men gave her a discouraging shrug of "Ugh, another woman; she's going to be trouble for us." Many didn't talk to her. She knew men who believed women were trouble for the unit. They felt they'd have to act differently around women, that they'd have to carry her bags, or wondered, "Is this one going to fall out of a run?"

Chrismer carried her own bags and then some. "I was always trying to prove myself, almost from the first day to be faster, smarter, stronger," she said. Frequently, she was the only woman in the workplace.

Over the past two decades, the Marine Corps has made strides to equalize careers for women. The physical standards have changed, and more operational specialties have opened up for women. Even the physical fitness tests are now similar, with the exception of the requirements of pull-ups for men and flexed arm hang for women. Before, women would run one and a half miles. Now, they run three miles as their male counterparts do, but the women score 100 percent if their run is completed in twenty-one minutes while the men are at 100 percent for eighteen minutes. "Of course, everyone knows women aren't as fast, but we have fast runners," Chrismer noted. "I just monitored two of my female marines running three miles in 20:08 and 20:40. So they maxed out their physical fitness test."

Chrismer's role as a drill instructor was to transform a civilian into a U.S. Marine in three short months. "As they get through the first two weeks of boot camp—the toughest part of the training—they begin to want to succeed more for themselves. By the time they complete the final weeks of boot camp, they don't want to leave the drill instructors who inspired them." Chrismer witnessed this repeatedly. "Many of them say it is the best they have felt about themselves in years, for as long as they can remember. Most of the time they can't even get the words out because their bottom jaw is trembling so bad. It's rewarding for the drill instructor when the new marine or her family grabs them and hugs them for all they have done to help. They don't realize their success is based on everything they did. We didn't get behind the weapon and shoot it for them. We didn't improve their physical appearance or ability. They did it themselves."

During the seventy training days, the recruits reinvent themselves. When they first arrive it is obvious to the drill instructors who has poor hygiene habits or who slouches. Others lack pride in their personal appearance, and some have little self-confidence. By the time they graduate, they stand taller and exude confidence, almost cockiness. "This is a good quality for women," explained Chrismer.

Chrismer regularly asked the recruits, by a show of hands early on in the training, why they joined. Only a few wanted to be marines solely for the education and money. Most ran from an abusive "someone." "The abuse is in many forms: from verbal to sexual, physical, even emotional," Chrismer revealed. "They look around to see that they're not the only one and realize that they are in this series [training cycle], with two platoons of young women that can relate to what I'm talking about and that they can't use having had a tough life as an excuse." This revelation develops teamwork; they pull together through the difficult milieu Chrismer describes as "kind of like prison." Recruits are told when they can eat, sleep, shower, and wake up. They all wear the same uniform and stay in the confines of the squad bay unless they are out training. The recruits are not allowed to go anywhere without a drill instructor knowing about it, for accountability purposes. The young women were scared. As the makeover began, they learned to lean on each other, to trust each other. They realized that the other women were feeling the exact same thing but just not showing it.

Along the way, drill instructors like Chrismer guided them in their journey. The attrition rate was low, surprisingly only 16 percent. Chrismer attributes that to the core values that were taught and demonstrated to them: honor, courage, and commitment. Additionally, great credit must be given to the men and women drill instructors of the United States Marine Corps. They sat down with their respective platoons to talk about things the recruits needed to be aware of before they graduated, including combat stress, policies that prohibit sexual harassment, and substance abuse. Periods of instruction also included infantry classes.

"Drill instructors of this day and age have the utmost respect for these young men and women coming in because they enlisted in the Marine Corps during a time of war. Recruits know what the inevitable is. There are more and more women going into combat. More than there were five years ago," she said. "These women know what they are going to face. If we can give them scenarios to start setting them up to think of what they'll experience, I think that is helpful. I don't want young women to think they'll never experience traumatic, stressful, chaotic times."

III

Operational and career fields for women are open except ground combat forces jobs in infantry, artillery, and tanks. The Marine Corps separates the men and women recruits during training to keep the focus on training.

Women and men are integrated in the field and they continue to serve in the Corps willingly, despite the realization that they are serving in a man's world. Chrismer admitted this. Debra A. Sharkey, a 1st sergeant in the Marine Corps who worked as a drill instructor at Parris Island with Chrismer, has also experienced the male bias.

Sharkey graduated from recruit training in November 1985. She was part of the last group of women to join the Marine Corps who were not allowed to use the shooting range in their training. Today women as well as men qualify as "marksmen," "in an attempt by the Corps to eliminate the stigma of a 'woman marine' and just have all defined as 'marine' in order to bridge the gap of differences," said Sharkey. Yet the good ol' boys network remained, even for the women who were warriors. Even though Sharkey later learned to shoot, she said female marines were treated differently by the military's male majority and culture.

A no-nonsense redhead, Sharkey's first mission specialty was operating heavy equipment and machinery. When she reported for duty it was with the Marine Corps Engineer Detachment, Fort Leonard Wood, Missouri. Subsequent tours sent her overseas to Okinawa, Japan, and the Republic of Korea. During these early assignments she was confronted with the different expectations given to "women Marines." "When I first came in, it was all about etiquette. It was all about what was proper," Sharkey said. "It was all about where a woman's place was." The conventional assumption that women did not measure up to men played out in everyday experience. Women didn't get the same number of uniforms as the men; even being issued a second pair of boots was unheard of unless it was necessary for their Military Operational Specialty (MOS). In addition, she was faced with a blockade with regard to work opportunities.

Although the heavy equipment operator field had opened up for women in the mid-1980s, few women were qualified. "I would show up on a job site as the forklift operator, and the supervisors were calling back to the office asking for somebody else. Before I could lift a box or move equipment, they just assumed I couldn't do it," she said. "They looked at me and laughed, like, 'You've got to be kidding.'" She drove the forklift, turned it around, and went back to the garage. "I felt like crap. Why am I going through this? I couldn't understand why I wasn't getting respect. I'm here to do a job. I haven't broken anything. There isn't any reason why you need to send me away," she said. "I think it was a male ego thing."

Sharkey was one of the pioneering women who had to fight to do the job she had been trained for. She and other women like her won by addressing the issues with their supervisors, which took bravery because the women were pretty insignificant when it came to rank. "We had to speak our minds, and lance corporals really don't have much say," Sharkey said.

Since her early career experiences, she acknowledged that the Marine Corps has evolved. "It's like a whole new breed. My forklift experience would not happen today, not at all. But women always have to assert themselves. We've all grown up, the men and women of the Corps, together as friends and fellow marines. We know what each other is capable of."

Sharkey has developed into a well-regarded leader. She has served in critical, high-visibility roles supervising both men and women. As a 1st Sgt. for

Headquarters and Service Battalion, she is responsible for providing uniforms, supplies, helmets, and food service for all the chow halls at Parris Island; the mostly male company had more than 260 marines and 200 civilians. An integral part of the chain of command, she was only one of four women leaders assigned to that unit.

As the 1st Sgt. she must make sure that the company runs effectively and efficiently. "Nobody is considered favored. Everybody is the same. Everyone gets treated fairly," Sharkey said. "I am responsible to hold the company to a higher standard."

Sharkey was also a drill instructor from 1996 to 1998, which required the completion of a grueling twelve-week course in preparation for the prestigious leadership assignment. "It taught me time management. It taught me how to be proficient under stress." Proven to be a top-notch drill instructor for recruits, she was one of the few enlisted marines selected to train officers in Quantico, Virginia, as a sergeant instructor for the Marine Corps Officer Candidate School from 1998 to 2000. "If I had not been prepared on the recruit level, I would have never been prepared for the officer level of training," she said. "Recruits, we baby step them up. You have to assume they are a group of people who have never done anything before as a group and work to get them to perform as a team." The prospective officers are expected to know how to create a sense of team.

For Sharkey, it was an experience like no other: "You have to be on your game up there. The people you are training could be your officers in charge one day. You have to be the one that taught them the right way to handle their marines once they get into that position."

Despite the fact that women were not permitted to serve in operational specialties designed to go to the front lines of a war, Sharkey deployed to Kuwait and then Iraq in February 2003 for Operation Iraqi Freedom with 180 marines and sailors under her charge. "It was scary, it was exhilarating, and it was exhausting. The thing I learned over there was that everything you'd been taught in the Marine Corps, no matter how small it is, it's all stuck in your head. Like how to protect yourself in a nuclear, biological, and chemical environment. All those things flood your mind when you are over there."

While in Kuwait, the reality of war first hit her quite unexpectedly. A nuclear, biological, and chemical alarm (NBC) sounded suddenly, signaling

NASA astronaut and U.S. Air Force Col. Pam Melroy wears a baseball cap from her alma mater while orbiting above Earth in the space shuttle—women astronauts did not exist in 1972 when Melroy chose her career. *Courtesy of NASA*

Col. Pam Melroy, launched from Kennedy Space Center as mission commander of the space shuttle *Discovery* on a mission to deliver "Harmony," an element that opened up opportunities for future laboratories to be added to the International Space Station. During the mission, Melroy met and shook hands with the first woman to command the ISS, Peggy Whitson. Melroy (left) still fondly looks toward the sky when she knows the ISS is passing above her on Earth. *Courtesy of NASA*

Ever since she was a young child, Nicole Malachowski dreamed of flying jets. With persistence, determination, and support from her family and friends, she made her dream come true. Lt. Col. Malachowski graduated from the Air Force Academy and earned her place in history as the first woman Thunderbird pilot. *Courtesy of the Malachowski Collection, U.S. Air Force*

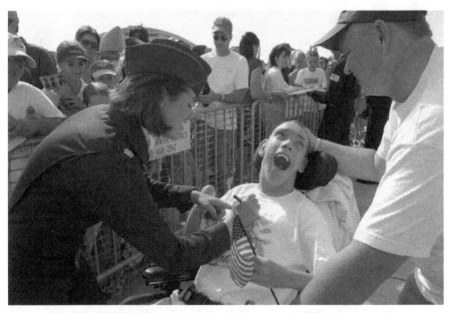

Following an air show at Hill Air Force Base, Thunderbird pilot Lt. Col. Nicole Malachowski signs a fan's t-shirt. Of the thousands of photos she has of her time as a celebrated aerial demonstration team pilot, "It's one of my favorite pictures," she said. *Courtesy of the Malachowski Collection, U.S. Air Force*

Command Master Chief Mattie Wells grew up in a small Louisiana town and rose to the highest enlisted rank possible in the U.S. Navy. Selected to serve as the commanding officer's enlisted adviser on three ships for back-to-back sea tours, she was a natural leader, proving that women are valuable leaders and critical members of the crew. Here Wells and her mother enjoy time together at a ceremony. *Courtesy of the Wells Collection*

Lt. Col. Tammy Duckworth, the assistant secretary of the Department of Veterans Affairs, shares a conversation with a World War II veteran at a ceremony honoring about 250 veterans at the World War II Memorial in Washington, D.C., March 10, 2010. *Photo by Alexandra Hemmerly-Brown*

Then president-elect Barack Obama visited the Bronze Soldiers Memorial at Soldier Field with Lt. Col. Tammy Duckworth on Veterans Day in 2008. Duckworth lost both her legs and partial use of one arm in the Iraq War. *Photo by John White, courtesy of the Chicago Sun-Times*

1st Sgt. Debra A. Sharkey enlisted in the Marine Corps in 1984 and completed recruit training the following year at the Women Recruit Training Command, Parris Island, South Carolina. She served in Japan, Korea, and Camp Lejeune, North Carolina and became a senior drill instructor and a series gunnery sergeant. She also deployed to Iraq for Operation Iraqi Freedom. In 2007, she returned to Parris Island for assignment as a company first sergeant—leading and mentoring women recruits to transition from civilians into marines. *Photo by Staff Sgt. Jennifer M. Antoine, MCRDPI U.S. Marine Corps*

1st Sgt. Brenda Chrismer, a member of the Combat Logistics Regiment Company, deployed overseas and to Iraq. "My life has predominantly been the Marine Corps," she said. "I have spent most of my time working well before the sun comes up and going home well after the sun goes down. . . . Sometimes, I do wish there were more hours in the day!" *Photo courtesy Staff Sgt. Jennifer M. Antoine, USMC*

1st Sgt. Brenda Chrismer served as a drill instructor at Parris Island, teaching, leading, and transforming civilian women into U.S. Marines. *Courtesy of the Chrismer Collection*

Capt. Cate Florenz Michaud (fourth from left) served as a series commander for women recruit training at Parris Island, South Carolina. Every twelve weeks about a hundred female marines graduated under her supervision and the instruction of female drill instructors (DIs). Pictured are DIs from the Fourth Recruit Training Battalion: Staff Sgt. Nickea Redding, Sgt. Beth Abbott, Staff Sgt. Helen Davis, Florenz Michaud, Gunnery Sgt. Venette Martinez, Staff Sgt. Yvette Wise, Sgt. Celina Arellano, Staff Sgt. Miriam Jenkins, and Sgt. Elisa Gaines. *Courtesy of Lance Cpl. Jon Holmes, U.S. Marine Corps*

Female recruits learn to become soldiers like their male counterparts. Being proficient at the weapons range is one of the essential components to graduate from recruit to U.S. Marine. *Photo by Staff Sgt. Jennifer M. Antoine, USMC*

Then 1st Lt. Cate Florenz deployed to Camp Victory, Kuwait, before traveling into Iraq to serve with the II Marine Expeditionary Force Headquarters in Camp Fallujah, Iraq, from 2005 to 2006. Later she left the U.S. Marine Corps and accepted a civilian position working for the federal government. She married Kurtis Michaud, an infantry marine in 2011. *Photo by Sam Chyung, www.samchyung.com*

A graduate of the University of Texas and commissioned an officer through Officer Candidate School, then Lt. J. G. Vivien S. Crea asked to serve aboard Coast Guard ships but was rebuked due to lack of female berthing. She then asked to fly. After steadfastly pushing for a change of policy to allow women to fly military planes, Crea was the second woman to enter Naval Aviation Flight School and earned her wings in 1977. "Never let anybody tell you 'no, you can't do something,'" she said. "That's not the right answer." *Courtesy of the U.S. Coast Guard*

Here, President Ronald Reagan arrives in Strasbourg, France with the first female presidential aide, Vice Adm. Vivien S. Crea. As a Coast Guard aviator, she flew the Lockheed HC-130 Hercules turboprop, HH-65 Dolphin helicopter, and Gulfstream II jet during her thirty-six years in the service. *Courtesy of The Ronald Reagan Presidential Library*

The first female to carry the "nuclear football" as military aide to president was Vice Adm. Vivien S. Crea. A highly respected officer and leader, Crea was also the first woman in U.S. history to lead a military service as the second in command—as the Coast Guard's vice commandant. Awarded the Coast Guard Distinguished Service Medal, Defense Superior Service Medal, Legion of Merit (four times), and the Meritorious Service Medal, Crea previously served as the operational commander for all Coast Guard activities within the eastern half of the world and commanding officer of two air stations—another first for a woman. *Courtesy of The Ronald Reagan Presidential Library*

U.S. Army Gen. Ann E. Dunwoody celebrates her promotion to general; as was tradition, she was pinned with her new rank by chief of staff of the army Gen. George W. Casey, left, and her husband Craig Brotchie during her ceremony at the Pentagon on November 14, 2008. Dunwoody made history as the nation's first four-star female officer. *Photo by U.S. Navy Petty Officer 2nd Class Molly A. Burgess, courtesy of the DoD*

During Desert Storm, Maj. Ann Dunwoody served as the division parachute officer for the 82nd Airborne Division. "A Dunwoody has fought in every American war since the Revolution," said Army Chief of Staff Gen. George Casey during Dunwoody's promotion ceremony in 2008. She said, reports the BBC, she was surprised and had never expected to rise so high in the ranks, adding, "Behind every successful woman there's an astonished man." Of the army's 500,000 soldiers, women make up 14 percent. *Courtesy of the U.S. Army*

Capt. Maureen Pennington finds some joyful relief from the stress of serving on the front lines in Iraq by playing ball with a Military Police dog. *Courtesy of the Pennington Collection*

[Right] Winner of the 2007 California State Women's Conference Minerva Award, Capt. Maureen Pennington celebrates on stage. *Courtesy of the Pennington Collection*

[Below] Master Sgt. Bertha Thompson discusses the plan of the day while on assignment in Afghanistan. *Courtesy of the Thompson Collection, U.S. Army*

Master Sgt. Bertha Thompson, an avid runner, races around one of sixteen loops during the Baghdad International Marathon held at Camp Victory, Iraq in December 2006. Thompson placed third overall female with a time of 3:40. The marathon was tougher than others she says because of the heat and traffic. "We had security personnel to assist in directing us but the vehicular traffic, possibility of indirect fire, limited water points, and fatigue from running after my night shift made it mentally challenging but not impossible," she said. *Courtesy of the Thompson Collection, U.S. Army*

The Air Force Academy's Association of Graduates presented its 2010 Distinguished Graduate Award to Heather Wilson, who served five terms in Congress. *Courtesy of the U.S. Air Force Academy*

Heather Wilson, Class of 1982, was the second female Rhodes Scholar from the Air Force Academy and the first academy graduate elected to Congress. *Courtesy of the U.S. Air Force Academy*

A military police officer with Headquarters and Headquarters Company, 425th Brigade Special Troops Battalion, 4th Brigade, 25th Infantry Division, provides security for a Traffic Control Point in the Sabari District of Afghanistan. January 21, 2010. *Courtesy of the U.S. Army, Photo by Sgt. Jeffrey Alexander, Pfc. Brialynn Lanteigne*

When Fidel Castro released prisoners from Cuban priso in 1980, the action culmina in the Mariel Boatlift, a mas exodus of Cubans for Amer soil on anything that could float. President Jimmy Cart accepted the prisoners into United States. In 1981, 2n Lt. Marene (Nyberg) Alliso was assigned to duty in For Chaffee, Arkansas during th incarceration of the Cuban refugees here. The prisoner that remained in Arkansas w held in the Fort Chaffee pri until they were relocated in a federal prison in Atlanta, Georgia. *Courtesy of the Ma Allison Collection*

Pictured here with her mother during a West Point Plebe-Parent Weekend in the spring of 1977, Marene (Nyberg) Allison graduated from West Point with the fi class to include women in 1980 and participated in th World Student Orienteering Championships in St. Galle Switzerland that same year. *Courtesy of the Marene Allison Collection*

Marene (Nyberg) Allison and fifteen of her West Point classmates received the Women's Foundation Hall of Fame Award on March 17, 2011, on Capitol Hill. Front row: Col. (Ret.) Terry Walters, Pat Locke, Robin Fennessy, Congressman John Shimkus (classmate), Liz O'Brien, Danna Maller, Joan Grey, Doris Turner, Col. (Ret.) Sylvia Moran, Mary Whitley, Kathy Gerstein, Kathy Silvia, Sue Fulton, Col. (Ret.) Deb Lewis, Col. (Ret.) Erin Misner, and Allison. *Photo courtesy of The Women's Army Foundation, provided by Marene Allison Collection*

Then First Class Cadet Sue (Donner) Bibeau excelled both academically and militarily at the U.S. Coast Guard Academy, a recognition bestowed on her with the authorization to wear both a gold and silver star on her cadet uniform. More than twenty years after graduating from the U.S. Coast Guard Academy with the first class to include women, Capt. Bibeau returned to serve as the academy's admissions officer. *Photo courtesy of the Sue Bibeau Collection*

Capt. Sue (Donner) Bibeau (right) excelled in sports at the Coast Guard Academy. She was the first woman at a military service academy to win a varsity letter— an item of note during an era when women were considered physically challenged. She proved differently. *Photo courtesy of the Sue Bibeau Collection*

Midshipman Belzer, a member of the Class of 1980, leads other midshipmen at the U.S. Naval Academy. *Photo courtesy of the Nimitz Library Special Collection Archives, U.S. Naval Academy*

"The novelty of being a girl is not the hardest part of being here. Just being a plebe is the toughest." Reporting in, Liz Sternaman (pictured here) arrived on I-Day 1976 with way too much gear, joining the first U.S. Naval Academy class to include women. *Photo courtesy of the Nimitz Library Special Collection Archives, U.S. Naval Academy*

Plebes learn the manual of arms. Pictured (left): Sandra Irwin, a classmate of Sharon (Hanley) Disher, U.S. Naval Academy Class of 1980. *Photo courtesy of the Nimitz Library Special Collection Archives, U.S. Naval Academy*

Sharon (Hanley) Disher, a member of the Naval Academy Cheerleading Squad and a native of Portsmouth, New Hampshire, graduated from the United States Naval Academy in 1980—the first class with women and men. She later married a naval submariner and had twins, Alison and Brett, who both graduated in 2010 from the academy. Her youngest son, Matthew, is a member of the Naval Academy Class of 2013, making the Disher family the first family whose members all attended the Naval Academy. *Photo courtesy of the Nimitz Library Special Collection Archives, U.S. Naval Academy*

Brig. Gen. Paula G. Thornhill entered the air force in 1980 after graduating from the U. S. Air Force Academy. Later she returned as an instructor and executive officer to the Dean of the Faculty. Thornhill earned her MA in history from Stanford University, PhD in history from Oxford University, England, MS in strategic studies from National War College, and attended MIT's Foreign Political and International Relations Seminar. Thornhill is a senior political scientist at the RAND Corporation and director of the Strategy and Doctrine Program within RAND Project Air Force. *Photo courtesy of the U.S. Air Force*

U. S. Navy Dive and Salvage Officer Capt. Gina Harden works on a hydraulic pump to lower the spider assembly arms around the USS *Monitor*'s gun turret in 2002. *Photo courtesy Phoenix Remora Remote Operating Vehicle, U.S. Navy from the Harden Collection*

As a student, then ensign Gina Harden qualified as a navy diver at the grueling Navy Diving and Salvage Training Center in Panama City, Florida in 1982. Her class was one of the last to train and dive in the MK V, which was then replaced by the MK 12. *Photo courtesy of the Gina Harden Collection, U.S. Navy*

that a deadly, invisible, airborne agent had attacked the troops. They donned their gas masks not knowing if this was a test, false alarm, or the real thing. She looked around to see if anyone was reacting to fatal NBC agents. It was then she noticed one of the young marines had slammed his mask on his face so fast it appeared he had broken his nose. The kid had also thrown up his breakfast in his gas mask. Although the NBC warning turned out to be a false alarm, the young marine's reaction brought home the differences between training and war. "In all the training we had done, nobody had actually done that," Sharkey said. "That was the realization that this was the real thing."

On the March evening when the Iraq War broke out, she was still in Kuwait with the marines. They were in their tents sleeping on cots when enemy missiles were fired toward the American troops. "When the first Scud missiles came in everybody went to the bunkers," she remembered. "When it was all clear, everybody went back to the rack [their sleeping cots]. Then we were right back out to the bunkers." The Scuds, dangerous ballistic missiles reported to be carrying the deadly NBC agents, would come about every hour. "I think the madness behind it was to keep us up all night. We were going from our cots to our bunkers, suiting up in all of our chemical protective suits and gear then taking it all off. Twenty minutes later everybody's back in the rack, minutes after that back to the bunkers," she recalled. "By the time daybreak came, it was all done with and everybody was totally exhausted. So we were kind of mad the rest of the day."

Recognized for her leadership in Kuwait, Sharkey prepared to deploy again in early 2005 by participating in Operation Desert Talon in Yuma, Arizona, with 250 marines and sailors in her company. Operation Desert Talon was a semiannual training exercise for aviation and support units deploying to Iraq or Afghanistan. Her company trained on necessary skills for survival in the war including convoy security, weapons firing, defusing simulated improvised explosive devices (IEDs) or mines, communicating with helicopters for medical evacuations, and helping service men and women get into the combat mindset before they left the United States.

III

As much as the Marine Corps has made great advances for its marines to serve equally without regard to gender in all mission areas previously restricted to men with the standing exception of infantry, artillery, and tanks, it is still a man's world according to Capt. Catherine Florenz. Florenz served as a series commander, a company officer who oversees the drill instructors and recruit training, with Sharkey and Chrismer at Parris Island. "Being a woman and a marine is a very hard combination," Florenz admitted. "Despite the Marine Corps' efforts to ensure that the Marine Corps is an equal opportunity environment, it is never going to be that way. It is a man's organization. And that's okay. If I were trying to create a war-fighting organization to be the most elite fighters in the world, I would not look for women."

Florenz believes that the Corps does not recruit females to serve as officers or enlisted. They simply tolerate women, provided they can pull their own weight. Considering the missions, she's fine with that point.

As far as dealing with the prejudice, Florenz constantly had to prove herself to navigate past the bias. She explained that when a new male marine checks into a unit, it's assumed that he's squared away until he proves otherwise. When a female marine checks in, the males in the unit assume there is something wrong with her until she proves she is smart, reliable, organized, and good at what she is trained to do. "It's certainly an upward battle," said Florenz. "There's always going to be that pressure. There are always going to be those females who are weaker, who are making this prejudice continue to exist."

Before being assigned to Parris Island, Florenz served in Okinawa, Japan, as a platoon commander in January and February 2005. Later that same year she deployed overseas for Operation Iraqi Freedom and was stationed at Camp Fallujah, Iraq. She worked as the reports officer, mostly writing situation reports twelve to fourteen hours a day for the Second Marine Expeditionary Force (MEF), the highest command level in Iraq. The reports would ultimately be cleared and sent to the Pentagon. Her most recent assignment was as one of six series commanders for the Fourth Recruit Training Battalion at Parris Island. According to the marines, it is the only all-female training battalion in the world.

Having deployed to the war zone, she understood the reasons for the challenges she and other women faced serving in the Corps. She described the bias: "It's based on the fact that women are weaker physically and the fact that they run slower. They are never going to do as many pull ups. They are never going to lift as much weight. This creates the illusion that they are all-around inferior, which is not true."

Besides the corporeal facts of strength, women can become pregnant. If they do, they are deemed medically unable to deploy. Some men in the military perceive being non-deployable as a physical weakness.

Meanwhile, looking at the differences in leadership styles, Florenz noted that women tend to lead differently. "The 95 percent male Marine Corps is going to resist that," she stated. "Women are threatening."

Florenz's feminine manner and professional appearance, though, was nonthreatening. An intelligent and beautiful blonde-haired woman, she also has a dynamic, mature personality with a witty sense of humor. Her career accomplishments and recent assignment, leading the drill instructors in their training of recruits, was a far cry from any assumption that as a woman she was not capable. In fact, Florenz exceeded the military's expectations of a great leader both at the training environment and during deployment to the combat zone. She oversaw the development of more than a hundred recruits trained by ten drill instructors, the ones who wear the Smokey the Bear hat and do the yelling. The officers, like Capt. Florenz, are selected for this assignment because they are some of the best in the Corps. While the drill instructors easily worked more than a hundred hours a week during the twelve-week training cycle, as a series commander Florenz would pull long hours, too. Her day began at five o'clock in the morning and concluded around six o'clock in the evening. She was responsible for the safety of basic training, the quality of teaching of combat skills, and the academics.

She kept an eye on the morale of the troops and quality of the instruction. Regularly she taught classes on the law of war and code of conduct and the policies prohibiting sexual harassment, alcohol abuse, hazing, and fraternization. "What they need to learn is to do the right thing all the time. They need to know that the reason they are here is bigger than just them," she said. "The most important thing is to keep their buddy alive and to be a person of integrity. That's what being a marine is all about."

She shared her belief about the situation minorities face no matter where they work: "I believe it is hard to be a female marine, and I believe there are inherent prejudices against which female marines are constantly struggling. But I do not think the struggle of female marines is unique; there are lots of minorities who fight for recognition in this and other fields. I do think the Marine Corps does a great job of affording females the opportunity to succeed. While the establishment cannot change the tendency of some men to assume the inferiority of women, I have never seen or experienced a denial of opportunity to any female marine. We fight for recognition, respect, and honor side-by-side with male marines, and only the best—male or female—survive. Most importantly, I think it is important to note that I do not think of myself as a female marine. I am a marine."

Florenz's leadership qualities developed naturally and over time, as would that of any officer or enlisted person. Growing up in Bethlehem, Pennsylvania, she attended public school. Her father was an attorney and her mother a housewife, caring for Cate and two other children. She described her childhood as fantastic. Her parents were very supportive. "They told me when I was growing up that I could do anything I wanted," she revealed. "I believed them."

She competed in high school cross-country and track, and still runs marathons with her father. When she was very little she was shooting guns in her grandfather's backyard. By the time she became a teenager she was quite a good marksman and became captain of the high school rifle team. She claimed that was her highest athletic achievement. "It was so much fun to be good at something where being a female was not a disadvantage," she explained. "There is nothing about a male's physical constitution that's going to make him a better shot. So it was an even playing field." Florenz was the best shot on the high school team and the only girl.

After high school, Florenz attended the University of Pennsylvania, graduating in 2003 with a bachelor of arts in German. "It is a great school, but I couldn't afford it, which is how I ended up in the military to begin with," she said. Her award of a United States Navy/Marine Corps Reserve Officers Training Corps scholarship in 1999 covered the costs of going to college. While enrolled in the ROTC program she decided to serve in the Marine Corps for a number of reasons: "I think largely for the camaraderie, the aura, and the big eyes people get when you tell them you are a marine, especially a female marine." There was another reason she joined the marines, she confessed. "I figured if I was going to do it I was going to do it right. The Marine Corps has the reputation of being the toughest and the hardest," she laughed.

"Whatever I'm going to do, I want to do the best. I wanted to challenge myself."

The world around her campus changed with the tragedy and shock of the September 11, 2001, terrorist attacks on America. Florenz had two years to go before she would graduate and be commissioned a second lieutenant in the U.S. Marine Corps. "When the twin towers were hit, I was sitting in college knowing that in two years I was going to the war zone," she shared. "I wanted to go. If I could have finished college early in order to go fight this war I would have done that." Her brother was already an officer in the U.S. Army. Most of her junior year in college she watched CNN's worldwide reports looking for him fighting for the United States of America in Kuwait.

Serving in the Marine Corps was something she loved. She joined the Corps to fight the fight. She knew the danger. "There is no longer any such thing as a front line. Distinguishing between combat arms and non-combat arms is almost silly," she said. "The people getting hit with IEDs are not combat marines exclusively. They are logistics marines, motor transport marines, supply marines, and communications marines, and women serve in all of those areas."

Promoted to captain when she was twenty-six years old, she served for five years on active duty. Looking back, the toughest challenge for her was the intense physical training during Officer Candidate School. Florenz was not sure she was going to make it through the six-week program. She had endurance but felt she was not a fast runner. Keeping up with the group was a real battle. "I can run an eight- or nine-minute-mile pace, and that was very much the back of the pack," she said. She practiced to improve her speed. Pull-ups, an option for women in addition to the flexed-arm hangs, were easier for her. She teased that she could do pull-ups all day. "The secret to doing pull-ups is doing pull-ups," said Florenz, explaining that doing them required the strengthening of back, bicep, and ab muscles. "I think a lot of it is how you are built. I'm built like a swimmer with a lot of shoulder and upper-body strength, more than a lot of women."

As a young officer she realized how challenging it was to lead. Like her male counterparts, she was put in positions of great responsibility for numerous people and equipment worth millions of dollars, with very little experience. As a second lieutenant and communications officer, she was assigned as a platoon commander. "I had zero experience, thirty-five people, and $5 million worth of equipment. I couldn't set up a communications network to save my life," she said. "Here I was in charge of setting up a communications station. It was a balance between relying on the enlisted members of my team who were the subject matter experts and being strong enough to make the decisions and have them be the final say." She believed that a lot of officers don't grasp this lesson and storm into a room saying, "'I'm in charge. You'll do what I say.' That's no way to win the respect of anybody."

By admitting to herself that she was not an expert, and with a little humility and some help from others, she was successful early in her career. Florenz relied on the advice of those who had been around a lot longer, yet she was strong enough to make decisions when the time came. She led her marines with strength and compassion, holding them responsible when they made mistakes but giving them another chance to do the right thing.

III

Florenz's decorations and personal awards include the Navy Commendation Medal, Navy Meritorious Unit Commendation, Iraq Campaign Medal, Global War on Terrorism Service Medal, Sea Service Deployment Ribbon, and Humanitarian Service Medal.

Florenz left active duty in 2008, transferred to inactive reserve, and then met her husband, a former marine who she married in January 2011. "It was never a career for me but rather an adventure, one thing on my list of goals," she revealed. "I'm ready to move on, but I've had a wonderful time. I wouldn't take any of it back."

Continuing her education, she is now a part-time graduate student at Georgetown University, where she is studying applied linguistics. She works as a civilian for the Office of the Secretary of Defense managing the Military One Source program, which provides military families, online or by phone twenty-four hours a day, a source to get help with a broad range of questions, from veterinary services to schools and child care.

Florenz Michaud is fond of quoting from William Ernest Henley's poem "Invictus" as a source of strength: "I am the master of my fate. I am the captain of my soul."

1st Sgt. Debra Sharkey was awarded two Navy and Marine Corps Commendation Medals and two Navy and Marine Corps Achievement Medals for her outstanding career of service and leadership. She retired in 2009 and moved to Florida after twenty-four years of distinguished service.

1st Sgt. Brenda Chrismer's future is very bright. Promoted to gunnery sergeant in 2006 and first sergeant in 2011, she was assigned to the Food Service Company, Combat Logistics Regiment-27, in Camp Lejeune, North Carolina, to serve as the company first sergeant for a combat logistics battalion—overseeing mission-essential combat service support and the well-being of the marines. In January 2012, she attended a five-week course for Senior Enlisted Professional Military Education in Quantico, Virginia. She was excited to hear that she was being considered to attend the Army Sergeant Major Course in San Antonio in June. Only three Marine first sergeants each year are accepted. Her personal awards include three Navy and Marine Corps Achievement Medals and a Navy Commendation Medal.

With her breadth of knowledge and leadership experience, Chrismer hopes to become the first female sergeant major of the Marine Corps. In this top enlisted role, she would help decide what is best for the Corps and act as adviser to the commandant. "My life has predominantly been the Marine Corps," she said. "I have spent most of my time working well before the sun comes up and going home well after the sun goes down." Sometimes she wishes there were more hours in the day.

6

Her Wings Broke the Glass Ceiling

Vice Adm. Vivien S. Crea, Vice Commandant,
USCG (Ret.)

From the beginning I couldn't accept "no" for an answer.

In 2006 Vice Adm. Vivien S. Crea became the vice commandant of the United States Coast Guard, second in command of an armed service under the commandant, Adm. Thad Allen. She was the first woman to achieve such a rank in the history of the U.S. military. Since her career began more than three decades earlier, Crea has been a driving force for revolutionizing the old-school mentality of a mostly male service to one of the most progressive, publicly trusted, and equal-opportunity military services in the world.

During interviews in May 2007 in her spacious office at Coast Guard Headquarters in Washington, D.C., Crea said, "Quite frankly, I never had the goal to be an admiral in the Coast Guard, much less vice commandant. My goal was always very simple: to do something I felt was meaningful, to make a difference, to continually challenge myself, to grow, and to have fun."

Was she gifted with brilliance to have excelled further than any other woman in the Coast Guard and of all the other military services in this position before? "I don't think I'm super smart. I think every person can put up his or her own barriers to the extent that it creates a glass ceiling," she said.

A tall, slender, and approachable woman in her mid-fifties, Crea is known for her winning smile and personality—both friendly and welcoming. Crea is committed to understand, to listen, and to help. She has earned the respect of all ranks and is humble about her extraordinary achievements. As we talked, she moved to sit in a neighboring chair opposite her desk, inviting questions. Behind her, a panoramic stretch of windows provided sun-drenched views of Washington, D.C., and the Anacostia River. Inside, mounted on pale blue walls, were historic Coast Guard maritime prints depicting dramatic, stormy, high sea rescues. Relics of the service's great history were also placed about the office. She described with a hint of pride how she recovered some of the beautiful pieces from storage, such as a brass bearing taker's navigational gear usually mounted on a ship's bridge wing. In this room full of memories and history, dating back to the Coast Guard's beginnings in 1789 as a well-respected sea service, Vice Adm. Crea told her story.

A glass ceiling did not stop her, she said, and her recognition from the United Service Organization (USO) as its 2007 Woman of the Year is evidence of that. Renowned men and women, including Caroline Kennedy and members of the New York press, applauded Crea during the celebration of her achievements at the Mandarin Oriental Hotel Ballroom April 17, 2007. Looking back at Crea's thirty-six-year career, it is clear that her impact was groundbreaking. Her actions redefined and opened up new careers for women serving in the military at a time when such women were few and far between.

When Crea joined the Coast Guard in 1973, men were not accustomed to the presence of women in their workforce. Only 10 percent of the students in her Officer Candidate School (OCS) class were women. The class, designed to transition civilians into military officers, was only the second one to include women. "The guys were great. I didn't feel any prejudice or lack of respect from the men. We all just helped each other get through," said Crea who graduated and was commissioned an ensign.

But at the time, Congress did not allow women in the Department of Defense to become military pilots, serve on board ships, be near a combat zone, or attend one of the five federal service academies: U.S. Military Academy, United States Merchant Marine Academy, U.S. Air Force Academy, U.S. Coast Guard Academy, and the U.S. Naval Academy.

When Crea applied for officer's flight school in the hopes of learning to fly military aircraft, and thus earning aviator wings in the early 1970s, her application was rejected because she was a woman. Since such policies restricted women's job opportunities and leadership potential, Crea challenged the denial.

She was not only appealing her application, she was taking on tradition and she had the support of other Coast Guard servicemen and the commandant of the Coast Guard, Adm. James Gracey, who felt that 51 percent of American talent could no longer be ignored. Her refusal to accept the status quo redirected the customary and regimented military mind-set. What was routine was legitimately called into question. The practices of the past had been viewed as acceptable and were even commonly referred to in both the corporate and military professions as the "glass ceiling." Crea said she was able to influence change, because "from the beginning I couldn't accept 'no' for an answer."

A little more than a year after graduating from OCS, Crea was promoted to lieutenant junior grade and faced a "huge fork in the road." She wanted to serve on a ship and fly aircraft for the U.S. Coast Guard but was told "no" to both. Instead of saying "Okay" and turning away from the goal and finding a new one, she approached the situation as an officer in charge of her future. She was the one who decided that "no" in this case was a problem.

"I chose aviation because the reason they said I could not go on a ship was that they did not have accommodations for women (separate berthing and bath facilities). It's a logical reason," she said. "Takes time, costs money, and there were not very many of us. I didn't like the answer but at least there was some logic to it."

In her appeal for flight school, she reasoned that a job in aviation was different from one at sea. The issues of accommodations did not apply. "So, I said 'No, wrong answer! I'm going to keep pursuing this,' and indeed it took a year or two to get the Coast Guard to see the light," she laughingly added. During the lengthy appeal process, Crea was assigned to work as a marine environmental protection officer.

Meanwhile, another woman completing OCS also wanted to fly. "I suddenly got this frantic phone call while up at the Coast Guard Academy, 'Get your flight physical updated; women are going to be considered this time!'" Crea and the other officer, Janna Lambine, were selected. Before leaving for flight school Crea asked to finish the important work she had begun in her current environmental assignment. In so doing, she became the second woman aviator to enter flight school behind Lambine, who graduated from naval aviation training at Naval Air Station Whiting Field in Milton, Florida, on

March 4, 1977. Lambine became the first woman military pilot to fly for the U.S. Coast Guard. Crea was the second.

"It took a while to break the restriction down, but it was breakable. By the time they changed the rules to go on ships, I was too senior to go, but being able to break that one down was a great winner," said Crea with a smile. On her uniform she pinned her "wings," evidence that she had indeed shined a light for the future of women in aviation.

Reflecting on her own experiences, she shared how her life was directed by her own choices. Now that she was allowed in the door, the trailblazer had to prove to herself that she could pass the rigors of the mental and physical stresses of flight school to qualify as a military pilot. Having only been a passenger in a commercial aircraft a few times, she admitted to not having a clue as to what would be required of her at the naval flight school in Pensacola, Florida. "I remember taking a flight aptitude test. I was by myself in a room and given pictures of different aircraft instruments and was supposed to interpret the information." She remembered sticking her arms out to her sides, trying to imagine what the pictures represented. "I'd never done that before, understood three-dimensional flight. I thought the instructors probably had a camera in there recording me walking around the room with my arms flying," she joked.

There were other tests and screenings. Some were psychological, and other physiological exams included physical tests of endurance and challenging obstacle courses. "I got stuck in what we called 'stupid' run or 'stupid' swim. If you didn't pass this one with fast enough time, you had to repeat. All in all, it was fun." One of the psychology test questions she had to answer was: "'Would I rather be stuck in the back of the bus and have to throw up or get my finger pinched in a car door?' I remember sitting there trying not to game it but figuring out what they were possibly looking for here. On the one hand, if I said I'd rather be stuck in the back of the bus and throw up on everybody, then I don't care about my crew," she recalled. "On the other hand, if I had said 'Oh, I'd want my finger pinched in the door,' then I'm a masochist. I'm still baffled by what the right answer would have been."

The flight school experience was exhilarating until the harshness of reality struck. "About two weeks into my flying, there was a fatal aircraft accident. It was a student with an instructor—they crashed. The student died and the instructor was severely injured. Suddenly, I realized these instructors were not *magical*. Instructors couldn't save every situation. *It was up to me whether I was going to live or die at any second.*"

Crea was scheduled for her check ride to determine if she was ready for her first solo flight the next day. She remembered spending the evening before "lying there in bed having sort of a crisis, thinking, deciding, *Am I going to be too scared to do this? Or am I going to be able to do it?*"

In this time of self-evaluation, she recognized that other people had flown solo before. She was as good as anybody else, and she realized, "If I knew my stuff and had self-confidence, what difference did it make if the instructor got out of the plane or not? I had, basically, the requisites in order to succeed. I'm not a religious person. But having that belief is almost like religion. It's believing in yourself. That is such a *critical* component of getting through tough times."

By the next morning she had worked it out in her mind, and she passed her check ride. From the experience, she learned a valuable lesson. "Periodically in life, you have your checkpoints or crossroads. Sit back and reevaluate everything. Hopefully, you've made right choices."

In the years that followed, her aviation career took off. Crea flew the Coast Guard's Lockheed HC-130—a Hercules turboprop fixed-wing aircraft—the HH-65 Dolphin helicopter, and a Grumman Gulfstream II jet.

Along the way she developed into an influential, respected leader who dared to think differently and act boldly. She was the first female commanding officer of a Coast Guard air station and commanded two of them during her career. Crea was also the first female district and area commander and was executive assistant to the commandant of the Coast Guard. "It doesn't take superior intellect to learn how to fly an aircraft or be a successful Coast Guard officer; it takes a lot of other pieces of a personality and character combined together."

Men and women who knew her during the tragic aftermath of September 11, 2001, remarked that she was the one they most wanted to serve with to accomplish the ongoing, changing mission of maritime security for New York and New Jersey. As the number of days until the New Year's Eve celebration of 2001 counted down, it was a particularly worrisome time. The Coast Guard's job, along with port partners like the New York Police Department, was to ensure the safety and security of the port of New York and New Jersey and to protect critical infrastructure from terrorist attack or harm.

The country was in a state of alert and at an increased threat level in the days leading up to the midnight hour celebration. It was a time of great uncertainty for the United States. Crea, as commander of the first Coast Guard district, was responsible for a vast geographic region and missions of national significance. The area encompassed the states and waterways of Maine down to New York and New Jersey. New York, Boston, and Washington, D.C., were particularly critical for Crea and the Coast Guard during this period because the September 11 attacks had deeply wounded the cities where many who served also lived and worked.

Crea knew she was in a position to make a difference: "I'd hightail it down to New York during a higher threat level. We would all sit there trying to come up with plans, how to resource it, moving small boats and crews, reservists, everything from all over the District and pile them up in New York. It was really just tremendously rewarding to be working with that team, which included Capt. Michael Moriarty [USCG (Ret.)], Cdr. Jim Munro, and Adm. Craig Bone [USCG (Ret.)] from Sector New York, as well as the men and women who worked around the clock to execute the plans by water and land. We have bonds of affection and enthusiasm for each other from working in this siege type of situation. I recall Rob Tarentino and John Healy [Coast Guard officers working for the District staff]. You'd come in at two o'clock in the morning, and they'd be up there plugging away, dealing with the operations. I will always cherish those opportunities."

Notably humble about her career and the opportunities it afforded, Crea was nonetheless an excellent officer, evidenced by the many high-level awards adorning her uniform. Of all these personal awards, which include four Legions of Merit, Crea is most proud of the Defense Superior Service Medal (Although, she is quick to explain that working a good search and rescue case means more to her than *any* award.). It represents one of her more internationally visible roles and probably one of her most challenging. The medal was awarded for her three years of service as a presidential military aide. In fact, she was the first female in United States history to hold this position. Crea was lieutenant commander during this prestigious assignment, working for President Ronald Reagan in the mid-1980s.

Once again it was a field she did not know much about. "She got the call to report to headquarters to interview for the position, but when she arrived, she discovered there was no way to prepare for the job and no job description to read. "I had the opportunity to ask a bunch of questions and pretty much it was on-the-job training."

The other military aides, one from each service, were the people she had to impress. They decided Crea would be a good addition to their team. "Five people filling one job have to be completely seamless, which means more than just your capabilities, experience, and background. Got to have chemistry, got to be able to act intuitively as one."

The position entailed three duties. The most visible was aide-de-camp, whereby the aide assists the president with awards, medals, and ceremonial presentations.

The second, providing military support for the president, is the most time consuming. Working with the White House Military Office and White House Garage, Secret Service, and White House staff, the aide coordinates military support for the president and staff when they hit the road for travel, whether it was to Camp David or around the world. The aide is the point of contact in advance of the president's arrival and determines requirements for provisioning and support during the visit.

The third role, and most important, was acting as the emergency actions officer for the president, staying close to his side so he could act in a moment's notice during a state of emergency. Military aides are always there, at the president's side or nearby, and taking turns carrying "the football," or the leather briefcase stocked with a classified nuclear war plan. They also assist with critical military command and control missions. "You try to stay out of the pictures as much as possible when you are carrying the briefcase," said Crea. "Not to the point of hiding in the potted palms, but always being close to the president.

"The best part of the job was working with President Reagan. He was an incredible, wonderful man. It was wonderful to be sort of a fly on the wall, see history in the making, watching top leadership and witness how politics work." Crea went to Bali and Japan, and had the lead advance and pre-advance trip planning for the European G-8 Summit.

While working for the president, she met a man who greatly influenced her life as her mentor. He was the head of the White House Garage and as an African American, he could identify with her struggles as a minority in the military. "He was an extremely inspirational leader, in a very, very nice way. He strove for perfection, challenged his people, but he mentored and cared for them as well—helped them develop the tools they needed to be successful. "Quite frankly, every once in a while, working in the White House as the presidential military aide, you get a little overcome by the politics and personalities of some of the individuals. I'd go visit him when I needed a time out and he'd say, 'Okay, let's put this thing into perspective.'" They'd sit in his office within the garage overlooking a fleet of vehicles or go across the street from the White House for coffee and talk. She learned that he had served as an enlisted man in the U.S. Army, rising to senior rank before transitioning to his civilian position in the garage managing the fleet of vehicles and limousines.

"You can find mentors who don't have to look like you. You shouldn't limit yourself in trying to find a lady if you're a gal, a minority if you are a minority. Just go find somebody who inspires you—has time to be interested in you and help you out." From his example, she also learned it was best to keep an even keel. It was necessary to focus on the big picture and have uncompromising standards, but also be able to forgive innocent mistakes. "I'm ornery enough. I don't want to do things because people say they told me to; I want to do it because I think it is the right thing to do," she laughed, adding that she used to have red hair and a temper to match.

By looking at situations from other people's perspectives and then trying to understand why they felt differently, Crea was able to maneuver across boundaries and excel as a leader. "It's not because you want to manipulate people, but you want to figure out how to make them understand so that they can make a choice."

By perfecting this style, a more collaborative approach results. Crea's preference was to assist "to the extent that I can help somebody feel that it is their own choice and it *really* is the best thing to do. Learning to think about putting yourself in somebody else's shoes is not that hard to do." She admitted that this effort takes knowledge of the subject, personal credibility, and integrity "so people feel you're not in it for your own self-aggrandizement."

Her leadership style and historic achievements have taught others about the barriers people tend to build as the excuse for not accomplishing their goals. "I didn't do things because I had the opportunity. I did them because

I wanted to do them." Her career was proof that women and men can attain what they want to achieve.

Before she retired from the Coast Guard in 2009, junior officers and enlisted men and women frequently approached Crea to say that they now know they can accomplish anything they want because of her example. "On the one hand, I find that a little distressing. I guess I was very lucky, I had parents that taught me that. But I think sometimes folks need a little kick of confidence: 'Hey, I don't have to be told no and accept it.' So to the extent I've helped that process out I'm proud."

Born in Fort Belvoir, Virginia, an hour south of Washington, D.C., Crea grew up with one older sister. The girls were U.S. military brats of adventurous parents who loved living overseas. The family had a great sense of stability even though her father accepted assignments that moved them all over the world. Togetherness created a tight nuclear family.

Every couple of years they would move. As a toddler she lived in Indianapolis and Fort Benning, Georgia. A few weeks after starting first grade, the family moved to France. Next, they lived in Germany and several other European countries before moving to the District of Columbia, where she stayed from fifth to ninth grade. "It's the longest I've ever lived in any one area so I consider this home as much as anywhere else." Before she completed high school, they were off again, moving to Korea and then the Netherlands.

A private person, she rarely spoke about the loss of her beloved father. He was a career officer specializing in finance for the U.S. Army. "My father was a very quiet, reserved, incredibly talented, and intelligent individual who was totally self-educated. You'd walk into the living room and he'd be reading a book on string theory or astrophysics or the history of music theory or back in his music room practicing the harpsichord for hours at a time—one of the several he had built himself," she lovingly recalled. It was under his direction she would work on the old family Jaguar and do "guy kind of stuff."

Crea is extremely close with her mother: "She still teaches me even though she's eighty-two [in 2007]. I learned how to age gracefully from her." Her mom was always a dedicated wife who took care of the home and family. Under her mother's guidance Crea cleaned and cooked. "My mother in her own right was a very independent, strong-willed person—she was determined that I wasn't going to get relegated to clerical type jobs," Crea shared. "She refused to let me take typing in high school so to this day I still type with two fingers. Thank goodness for spell check and word processors. I typed my whole 150-page thesis at MIT with two fingers! But it worked!"

Her mother's wisdom in keeping her unqualified for clerical jobs would change her future. "I was never able to take an easy out by saying I'd like to have one of those [secretarial] jobs. I had to go for one that required other skills," said Crea. "She was very strong willed—both of my parents told me to have high expectations of myself and never let anyone tell me I could not do something.

"My father refused to let me think that I did not have potential. My parents held me to very, very high standards. They had great expectations for me—not for any specific thing, just not to be lazy and to fulfill my potential." On one occasion she came home from school with a B on her report card. "It was the biggest scandal that had ever happened because I had let them down, let myself down." This upbringing instilled in Crea a great sense of self-confidence, a belief that she could do anything she wanted to do, provided she worked hard to achieve it.

Graduating from high school at the age of sixteen, Crea attended college in Munich, at an undergraduate school for military brats, and finished her bachelor of arts degree at the University of Texas in Austin. "We had a whale of a good time over in Munich," she remembered. "My mother used to say, 'You majored in beer drinking. Minored in Oktoberfest'—some nasty kind of remark—which was very true." Crea understood that education is partly about scholastics and partly about finding the right balance. She admitted that some of the choices she made after leaving her strict military family for the "unbounded freedom of college" narrowed her future opportunities. "I didn't have the grades to go to medical school because I goofed off and didn't study." Years later she would make up for it.

But first, she had to get a job. Her search began in Washington, D.C. She'd hoped to land interviews with the National Oceanic and Atmospheric Administration (NOAA) and the Environmental Protection Agency (EPA), but times were difficult. The federal government was in a hiring freeze in 1972. As an alternative, her dad mentioned that the U.S. Coast Guard had a marine environmental protection program and perhaps that would be a good place to start looking for employment.

She visited the Coast Guard recruiting office. "I didn't want to do the corporate stuff. I was a fish hugger, whale hugger, tree hugger," she recalls telling the recruiter. "I wanted to save the world." What struck her was the evident enthusiasm the recruiters had for their previous work out in the field, preventing and cleaning up pollution in the ocean and saving marine mammals and the environment. "They were making a difference, and they liked working with each other. Having fun with each other and doing really neat stuff. This is great! I wanted to do this. So, I signed up. Then I found out everything else the Coast Guard does," she said. It was the summer of 1973 when she agreed to a three-year commitment.

Later, Crea did improve her academic standing while serving as a Coast Guard officer. "It was very important to me to go to MIT because I wanted to prove to myself that I could excel in an extremely good school. I wanted to measure myself against that standard and succeed, which is why I picked the Sloan Fellows program." The one-year MIT Sloan Fellows MBA program she attended was for exceptional, mid-career executives. Graduating with a master of science in management was another remarkable win for Crea.

She found it striking to hear the five women in her class confirm their perception of a glass ceiling in the corporate world. "MIT is as frustrated as we are in that they don't seem to be able to attract women into their program. They [Crea's women classmates] felt there was a glass ceiling. I didn't feel that way at all. If there was something I wanted to do, I would do it." Crea hoped that by sharing her story and beliefs, she could inspire other women to rid themselves of self-imposed limitations. Crea does believe that women bring something different to the table. "There is a perception that we are more compassionate, more intuitive. That women are better listeners. Sometimes perceptions are as important as reality because people think that's the way we are going to be. If you are treated differently, you sometimes get access to more information and are able to help in a less threatening manner." And that's not all.

"I'm very lucky that I've been accepted into the ol' boys network but also have the ol' girls network, which is pretty unique. Before there were a lot of women in the military I got accepted by the spouses. The wives accepted me. I kind of had an 'in' with them. As with any minority, you often have a network just because there are so few of you. Not that you seek it out. It's just natural.

Particularly in a small community, like aviation, as more and more women came into aviation, you knew most of them at least by name. So you have that network, that communality with half the human race. That's nice!"

Crea is married and has no regrets serving her country. In fact, with the exception of a few frustrating days or extremely annoying moments, she never came close to thinking, *I'm going to quit*. Facing head-on the turbulence along the way with a positive outlook, she is delighted with her life choices.

There was only one thing she did not achieve. "I got everything I ever wanted—really!—except for the National War College because I went to the Sloan Fellows Program," she heartily laughs.

In the summer of 2008 Crea became the U.S. Coast Guard's twenty-first Ancient Albatross, a designation of honor for the longest-serving aviator on active duty. She was also the highest-ranking aviator in the Coast Guard.

How do you define leadership? Her definition of a leader includes "what you bring to the table—a sense of trust or integrity that people who work with you have in you that you know the job, add value to it, and are going to help them get to where they want to go in terms of mission accomplished."

Crea's passionate approach to life has given her much strength and courage. "It is very important to me that I could feel a passion for and a commitment to something which is relevant," said Crea of her service in the United States Coast Guard. She retired in 2009. With a bit of humor, she jokingly referred to the color of the uniforms in saying, "Always wear something blue!" Then in heartfelt words she spoke earnestly and gravely about her approach to life:

> You've got one life. You don't want to waste it. You have to find out what is important to you and you have to do it. You have no right to inflict pain or unhappiness on other people, nor do they have the right to do it to you—but, when it happens, get through it. It is hard, but you have a lot of choices. You are in control—you can decide if you are going to let yourself get eaten up by a situation or whether you are going to respond and move on, get yourself out of it, or take it on, head on. You don't have to just subject yourself to it. You are in charge—maybe you are not in charge of the other person, but you are in charge of what you do about it.

7

First Female Four Star

Gen. Ann E. Dunwoody, USA (Army Materiel Command)

I had never heard of the phrase the "glass ceiling" when I was growing up because my mom and my dad encouraged all of us to be the best that we could be in everything we did—that nothing was impossible with hard work and commitment. You just set your mind to it.

Gen. Ann E. Dunwoody was thrilled to have her soon-to-be ninety-year-old father, a veteran of three wars, witness her historic promotion to a peak never before reached by a woman in the U.S. military. Televised by the Pentagon and covered by international news media, the November 14, 2008, ceremony, documenting the first time a woman was promoted to four-star general, was seen by teary-eyed and cheering fans around the world.

Young girls sent her fan mail. One such letter from Ryan Marie (age eight) included a color photo of the child dressed in army fatigues, with four star collar devices, and rendering a salute. She wrote to Dunwoody, a thirty-three-year army veteran at the time, describing a school presentation she gave about the general's achievements. In neat handwriting she scribed, "I hope one day I can be just like you. I told my classmates you are an inspiration." Eleven-year-old Katelyn, from Spokane, Washington, wrote, "I think you are setting a good example for other girls like me. It shows me I can do anything I put my mind to." Isabel Demmon of Fitchburg, Massachusetts, and her twin sister, Priscilla, who served in World War II as an army nurse and a Coast Guard SPAR (women's reserve) respectively, wrote, "I am PROUD OF YOU for attaining this great honor. I am certain that you shall prove to be able to meet all challenges or you wouldn't be where you are."

Gen. Dunwoody serves among 214 war-tested generals and presidents who wore four stars, including Colin Powell, Norman Schwarzkopf Jr., George Patton, Dwight Eisenhower, Douglas MacArthur, and Ulysses S. Grant. Her advancement occurred forty-one years after general and flag ranks were opened to women. What did it take for a woman to achieve this uncommon, and perhaps to some, unlikely promotion?

While her father's army service in World War II and the Korean and Vietnam Wars took him away from home for long deployments, her mother's ability to raise five children alone made an impression on Dunwoody. It was extremely difficult, as Dunwoody finally came to understand: "I didn't realize probably until later in my adulthood what a hero my mom was. She was a role model for me." Her mother was the most selfless, gracious, and caring person Dunwoody ever knew, always taking the backseat and putting her children's needs ahead of her own. A graduate of Cornell and a home economics teacher, her mother worked, made the family's clothes, and encouraged them with optimism. Her take on life was that the glass was always half full—and no matter how tough the challenge, it was never going to rain on their parade. Those sentiments were infectious: "At the end of the day, if I could be more like my mom, I would be a better officer.

"I tell people that I had never heard of the phrase the 'glass ceiling' when I was growing up because my mom and my dad encouraged all of us to be the best that we could be in everything we did—that nothing was impossible with hard work and commitment," said Dunwoody. "You just set your mind to it."

The courage and commitment of her father also propelled Dunwoody through her uncharted career path. He was a man of integrity, had a sense of humor, and had honorably served his country for thirty-one years. Dunwoody learned a great deal from him, as a parent, a patriot, and a soldier.

She considered herself a tomboy growing up. "I could outrun all my boyfriends. I always loved sports, and I thought from a very young age that I was going to major in physical education and become a coach," Dunwoody said. In pursuit of this dream, in 1971 she attended State University of New York (SUNY) at Cortland, one of the top ten physical education (PE) schools in the nation. As her family also lived in upstate New York, it was a good fit in that Dunwoody could help her mother, who was raising the last two children while her father was serving in the Vietnam War. While at Cortland, Dunwoody participated on the tennis and gymnastic squads all four years.

It was during her junior year of college that Dunwoody was recruited to attend a direct commission program called the Junior College Program for prospective army women officers that would commission her in the Women's Army Corps (WAC). Although she grew up an army brat and her brother, father, grandfather, and great-grandfather had all graduated from West Point and a sister was a direct-commissioned army officer, Dunwoody had never assumed she would join the army. Nevertheless, she decided to take the opportunity the recruiters offered. The timing was key. It was the mid-1970s and women were now permitted to serve in an unprecedented new range of military missions—except combat roles.

The WAC, created to support the World War II effort and fighting men, began nearly thirty years before Dunwoody signed up. The roles and missions women could qualify for and serve in were limited by law, and females were not integrated into the regular army or reserves, although the WAC did permit women to serve in support and clerical roles with military status. Its predecessor, the Women's Army Auxiliary Corps (WAAC), an army auxiliary, did not offer military status even though the first WAAC members were sent overseas during World War II to Algeria, North Africa, and England. By 1943, the auxiliary was discontinued and replaced by the WAC. Its members served in New Delhi, India; Cairo, Egypt; New Caledonia; and Sydney, Australia, during the war. From a high of 99,000 women during World War II, the WAC decreased to about 6,500 women on active duty by May 1946.

Two years later President Truman signed into law the Women's Armed Services Integration Act, which permitted women in the regular army and the Organized Reserve Corps. The first permanent WAC training center was established in Fort McClellan, Alabama, in 1951. Basic training and courses in clerk-typist, stenography, and leadership were conducted for enlisted personnel, along with basic and advanced courses for officers. During the Korean and Vietnam Wars, WAC detachments were established in Okinawa, Japan, and Southeast Asia to support the regular army.

Promotion restrictions on women officers were removed in 1967, making it possible to achieve general officer or flag ranks. The first WAC officer to be promoted to brigadier general, a one-star general, was Elizabeth P. Hoisington on June 11, 1970. The army had its first brigadier general that same year—Anna Mae Hays, chief of the Army Nurse Corps.

To help the army maintain its required strength after the end of the draft in 1973, a major expansion of the WAC began. This resulted in a strong recruiting campaign and the opening of all military occupational specialties to women, except those involving combat duties. With the advent of the all-volunteer army, WAC numbers grew past 52,000 by 1978.

It was the end of an era and the beginning of a revolution when Dunwoody, a college student, joined the WAC. She met women from around the country. It was invigorating and exciting. As a college senior, she was paid $500 a month, a lot of money back then, according to Dunwoody. When she graduated in 1975 from SUNY–Cortland with a degree in physical education, she was commissioned a second lieutenant in the Women's Army Corps with only a two-year service commitment. Dunwoody reasoned, with her mom's optimism, that the glass was half full. This obligation would be a detour on her route to becoming a coach. However, being an officer changed the course of her life.

Dunwoody heard early in her commitment that women, for the first time, were being allowed to attend airborne school. The news grabbed her attention. She was determined to serve as a quartermaster officer. As part of the Quartermaster Corps, the logistical center point for all army operations, she would be responsible for making sure equipment, materials, and systems were available and functioning for missions—a supply support and distribution chain for soldiers and units in the field. She was also excited that they would teach her how to parachute. She thought, *Wow, that's really cool. I get to learn to jump out of airplanes, which is right up my alley as a physical education major.*

Even though she knew it was exciting, not everyone embraced women coming into the airborne community. When she went to her staff assignment at the 82nd Airborne only 2 percent of the soldiers in the entire division were women. Women were discouraged from having long hair. They were told it was too dangerous to jump wearing barrettes, and they should either cut their hair short or tape it to their head for their jumps before parachuting out of airplanes. Dunwoody opted for the tape. Stepping out the airplane cabin door for the first of many jumps, she did not become unglued by the interest her attempt provoked solely because of her gender. In fact, she was the stick leader, the first one out of the aircraft. She said her position in the line-up was because the instructors figured that if a woman would jump out, the guys would follow. Plenty of soldiers continued to follow Dunwoody's leadership, determination, and courage for the next thirty years.

What do we do with Dunwoody? was a question her supervisors asked when she reported for duty as a quartermaster officer in 1975. The men, unnerved by the rare occurrence of a woman under their supervision, doubted her capability to lead. The easy resolution was to assign Dunwoody the duties of property book officer, managing property and equipment. It was a low-level, limited-responsibility job. She was frustrated, but she worked hard and did the best she could. The men in her chain of command saw she had talent and soon recognized her ability to lead. Within six months, she was moved up and out of property management.

Later in her career she deployed with the 82nd Airborne during the first Gulf War as its division parachute officer, previously a male-coded position. She was also the first female battalion commander in the 82nd. "This was my journey," Dunwoody believed, and she admitted that if at any point she reached a crossroad where her talent and drive were not being recognized she would apply her passion elsewhere.

The transformation of women's traditional roles in the military to first-time service in male roles reflected a cultural revolution taking place as Dunwoody's career was getting started. Society and the U.S. military's ways of thinking about women's leadership and independence were changing forever with the all-volunteer army. Notions of what a woman could and should do as a service member were tested, fought for, and won. Women like Dunwoody fueled the revolution with authenticity and character.

Women entered the Reserve Officer Training Corps (ROTC) college and university programs in 1972. Four years later the first women cadets walked into the hallowed halls of the U.S. Military Academy, U.S. Air Force Academy, U.S. Naval Academy, and U.S. Coast Guard Academy. The first women graduated as commissioned officers from these military service academies in 1980. For three decades, a great revolution was taking place. The courageous women who took these first steps were supported by the men who believed they should.

Leaders within the military services and members of Congress understood the inherent need for women to be assimilated into the structure of the military. After all, they made up 50 percent of the workforce. Eliminating any feelings or appearance of separateness was critical. To help, the Women's Army Corps was disestablished by an act of Congress in the fall of 1978. No longer would there be a separate corps of the army for women; they would all be U.S. Army service members. Only the combat arms missions would remain exclusive to men.

Old societal rules needed to be abolished. The women's rights movement helped reverse the expectation that women were to stay at home, care for the family, and support their husbands. Until 1971, the U.S. Marine Corps would not accept the initial enlistment of a married woman. If a woman had had an illegitimate pregnancy, the Corps would not consider her enlistment either. A pregnant service woman or a woman who adopted was discharged from the military. Women marines and army soldiers were not considered riflemen and not trained to be warriors. Going to the range and qualifying to shoot a gun was prohibited. Women were banned from serving aboard navy ships, even the noncombatants. The Supreme Court ruled the inequities in benefits for the dependents of military women in the mid-1970s—military women with children or a spouse were not authorized housing benefits and their dependents were not eligible for medical benefits or commissary privileges—were unconstitutional.

Dunwoody understood that the formative years after 1975 offered positive opportunities to further the roles of women. It was her legacy to serve as one of the first females assigned to conventionally male responsibilities, such as division parachute officer and battalion commander, and to further the credibility of women as leaders. "What you had to do was fight the tendency for them to put you in charge of all the women," Dunwoody said. Standing firm with her conviction was not the easy path. It would have been easier to accept an assignment to lead only women. Instead, she insisted on a mixed gender platoon: "That was our role. Our whole generation of women came in at a time when we were responsible for helping to push the integration of women. We were making it a reality by not accepting the roles we had in the past. As a result, we had similar career paths as our male counterparts." The platoons were molded into companies with men and women serving together—something not previously afforded by the Women's Army Corps. Dunwoody and other female soldiers realized that challenging traditional roles at that time was an important first step to permit the changes needed to fully integrate women in the army.

Serving as an officer in the army offered her the honor early on to lead soldiers. "Even though I was only going to stay for two years at the time, I never turned down any job that might open doors," she said. "When my two years were up, I found I loved soldiering. I had hundreds of people under my responsibility and we did PT [physical training] every day. We ran every day. You led these soldiers. You learned from these soldiers." She thought, *Who on the outside world would ever have that kind of responsibility as a young person coming out of college?* Dunwoody knew she could make a difference, and she enjoyed it. After talking it over with her father, she decided to stay.

Leading and molding Dunwoody for her future during her years as a junior lieutenant in Fort Sill, Oklahoma, was Sgt. 1st Class Wendell Bowen. This was a significant period of change not only for Dunwoody but also for the service as a whole. Integration of women was one of the top issues. Recovering from Vietnam was another. "It was a hollow, kind of broken army," Dunwoody said of the challenges faced after the Vietnam War. "I was fortunate to have one of the very, very best platoon sergeants in the entire United States Army. There was nothing broken about him. He taught me what right looks like. He taught me how to be a lieutenant, a platoon leader. Because of him, my foundations as an officer were rooted in honesty, standards, integrity, passion, and caring for your soldiers."

She readily admits that left up to the military system, she might not be where she is today. "I'm very fortunate that people have given me opportunities. You know, if you believe in yourself, then others also believe in you," she said. Throughout her career she's had someone believe in her and give her a chance, an opportunity, and she has tried to do the same for others.

Other male role models guided her on her breakthrough journey. She didn't work for any women because there were none. She admitted learning something from everyone, but men set the example. Battalion commanders, division commanders, and army chiefs and vice chiefs of staff showed her how to be the right kind of leader. They demonstrated intelligence, personal courage, commitment, and dedication. Those were the leaders she aspired to be like. Dunwoody had the right-mindedness, dedication, courage, and talent to rise to the top. She led soldiers and excelled in command positions and key staff assignments. She received a master of science in logistics management from the Florida Institute of Technology in 1988 and a master of science in national resource strategy from the Industrial College of the Armed Forces in 1995. Recognized with the Distinguished Service Medal, Defense Superior Service Medal, Legion of Merit decorations, Defense Meritorious Service Medal, and Commendation and Achievement Medals, she continued to advance to the highest rank once thought not achievable for a female. "If I believed that I was nominated for this four-star rank because I was a woman, I would not have taken it," she said. "I believe I was nominated and selected because I was the best qualified."

Brig. Gen. Myrna Williamson (Ret.), who predicted the day would come when there would be a female four star, made a set of four-star earrings years before it happened. Williamson presented the jewelry to Dunwoody during a 2008 luncheon celebrating her history-making promotion at the Women in the Military Service for America Memorial in Washington, D.C. Dunwoody had imagined the event would include a few retired and active duty women who had achieved star rank. When she discovered there were more than seventy female flag officers there, she was astonished.

The accessory was not at all symbolic of predetermined fate or given success. Each of those in attendance had made a choice along their journey to sacrifice something for their own star; from the first woman to earn one in 1970 to the mid-1990s when women had begun to make three-star rank, they all had this commonality. Dunwoody knew what she had chosen to sacrifice. After she married Craig Brotchie, a combat controller and special operations air force officer, in 1989, they decided not to have children of their own. The army was her family. "Leadership is a contact sport. The higher up you go, the more time you devote to soldiers, civilians, and their families, often at the expense of your own family," Dunwoody said. "They will do anything for you," she said of the selfless service of those in the military. "This is a noble profession and we're in it to serve our country. We're very, very blessed that parents entrust the lives of their sons and daughters to our care. I think we owe it to them to provide the ultimate care and training, and that we ensure they are the best-led and equipped army in the world."

To see Dunwoody and the four stars on her shoulders is quite impressive. "They are kind of heavy," she smiled, "but I have a lot of help." Help also means answering the duffle bags of mail and hundreds of e-mails from her fans. "At first I didn't appreciate the enormity of it because this was our journey. I was just lucky and fortunate to be the first. The bench is deep and there are many. I may be the first, but I know with certainty that I won't be the last," said Dunwoody, humbled by the experience and celebrity. She was writing back, fifty letters a night, to World War II veterans and third graders across the country. She held up a sample letter, written on a nearly extinct typewriter, that included these heartfelt words: "I was a World War II vet. I want you to have my memoirs." "What I knew is that they all felt responsible for this journey," said Dunwoody. "It's not about me. It is about the step forward, so to speak."

With that step forward comes the demands on her precious time and the responsibility or obligation to reach out and reach back to thank those who appreciated her historic achievement. Dunwoody wanted to inspire others, give them hope. "You're right," Dunwoody often wrote in response to the admiring letters of praise, "you can be anything you want to be."

As a role model for other soldiers, men and women alike, Dunwoody wants them to know that the opportunities are there. The doors will continue to open for others as they have for her. "I believe that the next generation will do things that are unimaginable to you and me today," said Dunwoody, "Just as this was unimaginable to me when I joined the army—even unthinkable."

Dunwoody, fifty-nine, jokes that her current position, in 2012, as the commanding general of the U.S. Army Materiel Command (AMC), which underwent a massive move of its headquarters from Fort Belvoir, Virginia, to Redstone Arsenal, in Huntsville, Alabama, during her tenure, simultaneously assigned with her promotion in 2008, is her sixth "last job." She admitted questioning a new job offer in three ways: could she do it, would she love it, and could she make a difference? Her career was seemingly day by day and job by job, but she knew within herself that if there was "some point during this journey that I didn't love it anymore or that I didn't think I could make a difference, then I would have done something else." She believes all people should be the same way: "You're not here to try to be a general. You're here to try to make a difference." Dunwoody believes that people should love what they are doing, as that is the key to happiness and success.

AMC, one of the largest commands in the army, with 69,000 employees and "an impact or presence in all 50 states and in 145 countries," has a diverse and complex mission. The command is the army's premier provider of materiel readiness—technology, acquisition support, materiel development, logistics, and sustainment—to the total force, across the spectrum of joint military operations to provide "a decisive edge on the battlefield."

AMC supports the troops from the industrial base to the foxhole, Dunwoody explained. The job takes her around the world overseeing a huge network. She is responsible for a global community of men and women working around the clock with a $49 billion budget and the management of $92 billion in contracts. "It's a breathtaking organization," said Dunwoody. "All the logistics for this great army fall under this command."

AMC has played a significant role supporting U.S. military forces during the wars in Iraq and Afghanistan and continues to do so simultaneously with a surge of combat forces in Afghanistan and the drawdown of troops in Iraq. Assisting with a reduction of force from 50,000 in Iraq by the end of the summer of 2010 and pressing onward to the flag-lowering ceremony at Baghdad International Airport on December 15, 2011, AMC was critical to the ending of the war. "There were over 120,000 deployed military civilians and contractors at the high water point to help facilitate this. It's a great sense of pride that I feel about our entire work force," reflected Dunwoody, who watched a video of the closing ceremony and troop withdrawal.

During these two monumental events, Dunwoody's command was a vital contributor to the success of the mission—leading the responsible shift of equipment and ensuring the visibility, accountability, and movement of the materials to other areas of responsibility, including Afghanistan, or back to the United States to be repaired and refurbished.

Throughout this process, Dunwoody remained mindful of the importance of equipment accountability and visibility because of challenges in the past. "Remember Desert Storm?" she asked. "Iron-like mountains of equipment were coming back in thousands of containers. We didn't know what was in them. We had to sort it out. We couldn't afford to do that this time." One success she pointed out was that 50 percent of the goods required in Afghanistan for the surge came out of Iraq: "That means we didn't have to buy it, and we didn't have to ship it from the United States." Yet as remarkable as the improvements have been since Desert Storm, with the updating of tracking systems and the investment in technologies, critical needs still remain. "If we had a weak sister, it was technology," said Dunwoody. "We were going to have to have a global transportation network. We never invested to make that a reality." Despite improvements, some of those same challenges they faced during Desert Storm surfaced again with Operation Iraqi Freedom a decade later. "We've been playing catch up," said Dunwoody, who had her team working with the best technologies to fine-tune the transportation network.

Dunwoody's team takes pride in ensuring American war fighters have the equipment they need, when they need it. One of the ways they accomplished this was by sending AMC teams overseas to assess equipment and quickly determine its usability. This efficient management of materiel helped ensure American troops had the equipment they needed in a much more timely manner.

> Where Soldiers are, AMC has a presence. I'm sure you've heard the saying—if a Soldier shoots it, drives it, flies it, wears it, communicates with it or eats it, AMC provides it. . . . We have tremendous capabilities in this organization. We use leading edge science and technology to give our men and women in uniform the greatest capability. This is an organization that touches a Soldier in every way.[1]

AMC responsibilities include managing the chemical munitions storage and the demilitarization and destruction of those stockpiles, managing the foreign military sales of equipment for our allies around the world, developing state-of-the-art technology solutions for our war fighters, and providing a vast array of contracting services and support.

Besides supporting a war on two fronts, AMC also helped with humanitarian missions in Pakistan and Japan. When the world witnessed the devastating destruction of the 2010 earthquakes in Haiti and Chile, Dunwoody offered relief to these stricken countries by directing AMC contractors early on to assess how they could help with recovery.

Reflecting on the future of women's roles in the military, Dunwoody predicts that doors will continue to open. "I think what you see every day is the incredible performance of women at all levels and on all battlefields," says Dunwoody. "Protecting, defending, saving lives out on the front lines—receiving Silver Stars. It just makes you so proud."

---

1 Kari Hawkins, "Meeting Demands of Changing Army," *Army.Mil*, January 4, 2012.

Where are women in the military headed, what doors need to be opened? Dunwoody says it's hard to quantify or define these next steps. Women have demonstrated they are capable and can do their job. "They don't want to be excluded when we go to the fight," Dunwoody says.

The future includes women serving on submarines or perhaps environments where they have been excluded. She feels that it is important to make sure the service is getting the best out of each and every soldier. "I think the thing that pushes that envelope is the talent," says Dunwoody.

Talented women committed and up to the task made the integration of women into the military seamless, Dunwoody said. The challenge now is the asymmetrical battlefield. Today's soldier does not have the linear battlefield of the past. Front lines and safe havens in the rear do not exist. "Folks like myself who were in the rear area supporting those on the front lines were not as at risk or life-threatened," said Dunwoody. "Now, we're on this asymmetrical battlefield where everyone is a rifleman first. You must know how to survive in order to support."

The battlefield today is dangerous. Dunwoody sees to it that today's army invests in training to this new mind-set by teaching all soldiers finance, adjutant general, and quartermaster skills, and how to defend and support. It's a hybrid war and counterinsurgency warfare eliminates clear lines of what's safe and what's risky. To train for this is very different. She says that providing capable men and women who've adapted to this new irregular warfare leads to "a very potent capability where you don't have to separate soldiers. We can use soldiers across the battlefield." With this hybrid type of warfare, all branches of the military train both women and men to adapt to all levels of risk anywhere on the battlefield.

For women coming along in the ranks, Dunwoody offers this advice: "Find your passion." She thought hers was going to be PE and coaching, but it turned out to be soldiering. "I do believe that if you're living your passion you look forward to coming to work every day. You feel so blessed that you're able to do something you really love doing," says Dunwoody. "I think you can't let people get in the way of your passion or your dreams. There will be folks that try to say you can't do that or you won't go there and you've just got to say, 'I can do it. . . .' At the end of the day, if you follow your passion you'll do stuff that you love to do."

8

Courage on the Front Lines

Capt. Maureen Pennington, USN

Don't be afraid to try something different. You always learn.
You become an expert, and then you do something different and
become a novice all over again and work your way up.
It still winds up teaching you so many valuable lessons.

The so-called Sunni Triangle, a densely populated region of Iraq, was a region of intense resistance to the American-led occupation first during Operation Iraqi Freedom, also known as the Second Gulf War, which began in March of 2003; then during Operation New Dawn in 2010; and through the end of the war in December 2011. Despite efforts to oust insurgent leaders with allied forces during the war, the constant barrage of attacks, bombings, and gunfire killed hundreds in ongoing battles. The region was considered a staging area for terrorist activity against U.S., allied, and Iraqi security forces, constituting an endless "triangle of death."

Car bombs driven by suicide bombers destroyed streetside shops and cafés or exploded near hospitals, turning whole blocks into rubble. A second or third attack would follow, aimed at the first responders who had quickly rushed in to help the wounded. Regularly, U.S. convoys were destroyed and their bases hit by rockets or mortars and gunfire.

For three years after the 2003 U.S.-led occupation, Ramadi, a city of 400,000 that lies along the Euphrates River about seventy miles west of Baghdad and within the southwestern angle of the triangle, was still very dangerous, not only for the combatants but also for the civilians caught in the crossfire. The wounded were brought into one of three surgical units located within the lower regions of the triangle.

Cmdr. Maureen Pennington, U.S. Navy, volunteered for the assignment to serve as the officer in charge of these units. She was the first Navy Nurse Corps officer ever to be appointed as commanding officer of medical surgical units. She rolled up her shirtsleeves and led the doctors, nurses, hospital corpsmen, and marines from February to September 2006 as the commander of Charlie Health Services Company, part of First Marine Logistics Group, First Marine Expeditionary Force, from Camp Pendleton, California.

The medical clinics were located in Fallujah, Ramadi, and al-Taqaddum Air Base (known as TQ)—"hot" zones that were prone to take enemy fire at any time. Each unit was set up as emergency rooms in tents or structures only ten minutes by helicopter from the battle zones. Around the clock, corpsmen performed life- or limb-saving resuscitation and treated sniper shots and burns or injuries from improvised explosive devices. Pennington, who had a background as an operating room (OR) nurse, faced things she'd never dealt with before. "I saw so many young marines dying, their buddies gathered around saying their last good-byes. I get emotional; please don't take that as a weakness," she said during an interview. She was reminded of a particularly painful memory of a unit commander coming into the clinic to find his four marines. One had been killed. Pennington's team was diligently trying to save the three others. "I had to tell him that his marine had passed. I remember him looking at me and saying, 'Maureen, you cannot give me one ounce of fucking pity right now because I'll lose it and I can't have it.' He wanted me to be strong and say, 'Go get your team together and tell them what's going on. Move on.'" She was also emotionally upset by the news but remained strong so that the unit commander could leave composed.

Pennington, who had deployed for eight months aboard the USNS *Comfort* (T-AH20) as an operating room nurse in the 1990 Persian Gulf War in Operation Desert Storm/Desert Shield, was now responsible for more than two hundred men and women assigned to the three trauma centers that comprised the largest surgical company in Iraq. She believed her background as a perioperative nurse led the way for her to become a stronger leader and accept the command assignment with confidence. It was all about the team.

"I learned to work with doctors and surgeons, making a whole team run in an OR. If you can do that, you can make anything happen," she said. Working in a combat zone was exceptional in many ways.

Her three surgical teams were each unique. Ramadi was all men because there was no berthing for women. She described them as a small, tight-knit group. The staff at TQ was more adventurous and innovative. Fallujah was a bit more formal because it was co-located with the senior leadership. "You think we all trained the same, all had the same roles, and then of course we'd all do things the same." Pennington said. "Absolutely not. It's the dynamic of the group that's there at the time which is going to set how they handle triage." Rather than try and force the teams to fit one style, she appreciated their differences. She was amazed to see that three distinctive places could do things three different ways and still get fantastic results. "There's more than one way to make it happen."

The differences in team dynamics were apparent every day in Iraq and each day was unlike any other. The teams took care of whatever came their way. They could be treating injured insurgents, prisoners, contractors, children, civilians, or American soldiers. At any time of day or night they could receive a radio call informing them that patients were inbound with an estimate of the severity of the injuries. They would not know how many would arrive or how they would get there. It could be by air or by military ground assets, like a Humvee or tank. Some would even walk in. At times the tension was just about unbearable, said Pennington. "Occasionally we ended up caring for someone who had injured one of our marines," she said. "I had to help my teams realize and remember that we were there to treat anybody that comes through our door." As humanitarians they had a duty to treat all people, even the enemy, as lives worth saving.

Sometimes she was angered at the sight of so many injured. As the leader, she forced herself to separate her emotions from her duty, especially if it meant coping with the overwhelming sight of death or the aftermath of fighting to save a life. Most of the population they treated was young, between eighteen and thirty years of age. "Watching these marines fight for life, they were just so strong," she said. "They wouldn't leave one another." Pennington's coworkers diligently strove to help them live. They also kept service members informed on how their fellow marines were doing as the hours progressed, sometimes to the point of letting them watch the resuscitative care because they needed to see that all that could be done was being done to prevent death.

One of the challenges was constantly maintaining a clean surgical setting—one that was ready to accept new patients at any time. During her tour in Iraq, more than 3,600 patients were treated. More than 600 patients required surgery and 760 were medically evacuated for more advanced levels of medical care. Despite many patients suffering from severe blast wounds from IEDs, Pennington and her team maintained an unprecedented combat-wounded survival rate of 98 percent.

Charlie Company also had to be prepared to handle large-scale casualties. In fact, Pennington and her team were barely on the ground in Iraq for seventy-two hours when their first mass casualty occurred. It was a critical test for them. Eighty percent of her team had never been there before. They were alone on watch because the group they relieved had left, so the newcomers were all that was left to carry on. Facing them were the urgent needs of twenty badly injured people. "I remember everyone kind of looking at each other for about five seconds and thinking, *Oh man, this is really it.* Then all of a sudden to watch the training go into action was incredible. The team got better every time. It was really like an orchestra in a lot of ways," said Pennington.

Pennington's units were also under indirect fire. Bullets were coming in close to their surgical area. During that first mass casualty, Pennington got a call that TQ had been hit. Three of her people were hurt. That was all the information the caller could give. They were a small group of men and women, and they all knew each other. "I had to bring my staff together and say, 'I'm sorry I can't give you more information but this is where it is right now and I'll keep you updated.'" They would learn that one of her nurses and two corpsmen were injured from the insurgent attacks on TQ. Later, the injured service members each received the Purple Heart.

Working to save lives on the front lines could have been overwhelming for anyone. "I felt like I had to be very strong. When other people were nervous, I couldn't be because I was the leader. I always had to make sure my team saw confidence in me." Based primarily in Camp Fallujah, headquarters for many of the operational decisions, Pennington put herself at increased risk traveling from there to each of the surgical units every other week to meet with her teams and to find out how they were doing and what they needed. The journey could take twenty to thirty minutes by helicopter or up to an hour and a half by convoy, an option she rarely took. It was a lawless country, one where they never quite knew what was going to happen or when they might take enemy fire. "I know it sounds crazy," she said, but they got used to it.

The stresses of the job, the constant round-the-clock delivery of injured, and witnessing the suffering were further compounded by being far from home and loved ones. Living in a war zone, it was normal that emotions reflected the unpredictable nature of their environment. "You're proud to be there serving and caring for your fellow service members. But you get angry. You miss your family. You see death and watch peers say good-bye to their buddies that have been killed," she says. "It tears you apart."

Pennington managed to appear to be standing strong despite the times she felt emotionally weak inside. "I'm a very emotional person. I cry watching sad movies or television shows when someone wins sixty thousand dollars. I had to learn to be a bit stronger out there." It was hard for her. She found ways to cope while also helping others manage. "Being a woman I had a lot of people come to me and talk about things that I normally don't think they would have." She assumed that if there were a male commanding officer there instead, the people who came to her for understanding and compassion might not have shared how much they missed their kids or their family. Instead, she guessed, they might have gone to their friends but not the commanding officer. Part of it was because of who Pennington is as a person. She can read people well and cares about helping them. The other part was because her office, located at the end of a hall, offered a sanctuary. "That's where a lot of individuals in my unit would come in and say, 'I need to talk to you for a few minutes.'" They knew it was safe. Some of the people she helped were senior officers in positions of leadership. She was viewed as the person they could go to when they needed to talk, and she loved that role.

Managing her needs was tougher. "In all honesty, I looked for things at the base that made me relax and made me happy." One of these happy things was playing with the dogs that worked in the K9 unit; when she needed a break she'd go see them. Another joy was visiting a small pond with ducks. "It brought me back to home. It made me feel safe."

Maureen went to the war zone leaving behind her husband and fourteen-year-old daughter, Grace, in California. Her son, Travis, twenty-five, was working in Antarctica for the technology company Raytheon. At the time of her Desert Shield/Storm deployment in 1991, Travis was only six and unaware of the dangers of his mom's assignment. Her 2006 assignment as the commander of the Charlie Health Services Company would be different. Her husband, who had served in Vietnam, was a steady source of support and understanding. She was able to talk by telephone with her family and reassure them, but that did not dissolve the anxiety her daughter felt, aware of the dangers her mom faced, watching much of the bombings of buildings and military vehicles from television news channel broadcasts or by reading about it in the newspapers. Her daughter's awareness and fear would haunt Pennington once she returned home, but for now she needed to focus on her mission.

The efforts to save lives in the wartime environment were experiences that created a sense of family among service members that went beyond the medical teams to include the military personnel in neighboring units. They all started to see a lot of the same people. "One day we might see someone bringing someone in, and a month or so later after we'd seen them so many more times, they might be brought in for treatment for their own wounds," Pennington said. "When we needed to be taken care of, they took care of us with supplies and made sure we had what we needed because they were so appreciative of our care."

Pennington improved the capability and success of her units by figuring out a way to get supplies on hand much faster than before. By working with the logistics personnel, they sped up the delivery process by utilizing software applications. They adopted a tracking system to increase the availability of supplies from fourteen hundred to five thousand line items. The turnaround time was astonishing. Before, the arrival of supplies could take an average of seven to twelve weeks, but they got it down to nine to fourteen days. They also set up an internal tracking system to visualize where in the supply chain the needed items were located. The marines took care of getting it all there, all the while operating in an unforgiving combat environment. The Bronze Star citation Pennington was awarded for her leadership and dedication to duty noted these achievements along with "her dedication to excellence in combat casualty care which established a benchmark for medical support of Marine combat operations."

"I know my name was on that award, but it truly represents the team. We were recognized for our willingness to be there, to adapt." Pennington felt guilty for being recognized with an award. She did not believe she deserved such a high honor. The Bronze Star was rarely awarded to medical personnel and Pennington felt there were many people who did so much more and were deserving of the recognition.

Before Pennington volunteered for the job in Iraq, she turned to her husband, who had served in the military for thirty-six years, to help her prepare for the assignment. One of the Coast Guard's original rescue swimmers, Dan Pennington enlisted and had worked his way up the ranks to commander. When she passed all the interviews and was going to be selected for the job, he sat down with her and shared from his experience what it was really going to be like to be a commanding officer in combat. "He asked me, 'Maureen, what if one of your sailors was killed? Have you ever written a letter home?'" she said. "All of a sudden, every bit of excitement I had, the reality of what you are faced with there and what you had to do, hits you. Was I ready for all of this?" He gave her sound advice: "Always listen to your people, communicate, train, and always think two levels above—like your two immediate bosses—and two levels below. You'll always have the right answers."

He also cautioned her about balancing her work with her desire for achievement. He said, "Maureen, don't chase success out there. Let success chase you. Do your job. Make sure your people feel ready and watch your people. When things go right they get all the credit. When things go wrong you stand up and take every bit of that blame. Don't let anyone mistreat your people out there. You take care of them." She must have had his advice in mind the third day she was there—the first time a mass casualty became her team's responsibility. He had cautioned that such a situation would cause everyone to have that deer-in-the-headlights look. He told her she could not, she needed to have strength. "You have to be somebody they can look at to know that everything is okay," she recalled.

Pennington and her team were a success. They all came home alive. But she was a changed person. This wife and mother of two realized that she was a strong naval officer and a stronger person within. Pennington and her team saw a lot of tragedies, a lot of death, but they also made a difference at every moment in the lives of others. "I saw heroes everyday," she said. "What people do during wartime in a combat area is amazing." She understood what must have happened to veterans in World War II and Vietnam and the experiences they returned home with meant that, like her, they must have been transformed. "You are stronger for the experience, but you also come back a little quieter because you reflect on the things that happened out there."

Coming back home was harder when she realized how much her daughter had anguished and stressed about her safe return from Iraq. "It was like running up against a brick wall," she said of the moment during the family's car ride home that Grace, a normally very stoic teenager, was suddenly sobbing uncontrollably. "It hit me, the enormity of how much she went through," Pennington cried. "Grace and my parents were worrying so much for my safety. I was focused on the mission. I didn't realize what they were going through for me."

Pennington said the entire experience in combat made her so much more appreciative of everything in her life. In 2007 she was awarded the Minerva Award by the first lady of California, Maria Shriver, during the Women's Conference in California for being a remarkable woman with a remarkable legacy. "Her work in Iraq, along with her two decades of active duty, offers living testimony to the difference one individual can make building a career out of serving the needs of others," wrote Caroline Kennedy for *Time* magazine. Pennington was the first military member to receive the Minerva Award.

The recognition gave her pause. *How did I get my passion for always wanting to face a challenge, to be a nurse?*

Pennington grew up in Maine, near Sebago Lake, in a small rural town called Naples. The dirt streets filled with tourists in the summer. She was an only child, and her mom stayed at home while her father worked in a paper mill. Her parents organized annual hikes on Mount Washington in New Hampshire. By the time she was ten years old she did her first climb. It was not an easy climb up Mount Washington. Her father and mother taught her a lot, especially about not giving up. Her mother could read people pretty well and knew when they needed encouragement. "Everybody who wanted to quit for some reason, she could talk them into going up that mountain. They didn't even know she was doing it," says Pennington. Her father took a new trail every time they went up. He said, "There's more than one way to climb a mountain, Maureen. Just because you climbed it one way, why would you want to do that again?" He taught her to appreciate nature, know her surroundings, and be attuned to them. She learned something different every time. Her foundation for being adventuresome was established.

By the time she was a sophomore in high school she had learned how to meet a challenge head-on. Loving an adventure, she decided to climb Tuckerman Ravine, a glacial cirque on the southeastern side of Mount Washington, a challenge she had heard about on hikes growing up and was determined to accomplish one day. With skis strapped on her back, she hiked up and skied down. Around that same time a friend took her on a seaplane ride over Sebago Lake and she experienced landing on the water and at the airport. After that, she announced to her parents that she was going to take flying lessons.

Her parents, who always permitted their daughter to express her thoughts as long as she was respectful, gave the fifteen-year-old permission to take lessons but cautioned, "Just don't ask us to go watch." In this instance, at least, they were not as daring as their daughter was. Having been brought up during the Depression, they were accustomed to going to work, doing their job—not traveling. That was something Pennington wanted. To pay for her flying lessons and her travel, she started working.

Her first job as a teenager was waitressing at a doughnut shop. By the time she went to college she had had quite a few job experiences, but the one that meant the most to her was working a couple summers at her father's paper mill, where he worked for forty-five years. "Let me tell you, that was an eye-opening experience," says Pennington. "It was hot and hard work. I was the college kid who thought I knew everything. What I learned there was a very valuable lesson. Many people who worked there had not finished high school, but I learned the value of humor, of common sense, and that education was not everything."

What she considers the most difficult period of her life was being a single mom in college. After she moved back home to live with her parents, who helped her raise Travis, she worked many jobs, tried to study, and took out loans to pay for her college classes. "I think sometimes you feel you can do anything and it's not anything big when you actually do it. You always look back at the times that were tough and realize, *God, if I can get through that many years or if I can climb Mount Washington or if I could ski Tuckerman's when I was a kid, I can do this.*"

Pennington graduated from Saint Joseph's College in Maine with a bachelor of science in nursing in 1986. Though nursing had not been a lifelong calling, she had found her interest in taking care of people while on the mountain as a teenager. Inspired by Marilyn Build, a nurse who helped care for the terrible blisters Pennington would get on her feet and also took care of other hiker's cuts, Pennington would go along with Build and learn how to care for people.

The same year she graduated from Saint Joseph's, the U.S. Navy gave Pennington the choice to take a different route. The new graduate was interested in the military. It offered travel, adventure, and a profession. "That was something good for a single parent, the job offered a lot of interesting things I was drawn to," she said. The first person in her family to join the military, she had to leave Maine and drive to Boston to seek out a recruiter.

Pennington was thrilled with her choice to serve in the U.S. Navy. As a junior officer, Pennington had the opportunity to volunteer for annual missions to third world countries with Operation Smile—an organization that helps treat children with facial deformities. The experience was so rewarding that she continued working with the organization for the next four years.

After twenty-one years in the service, Pennington was promoted to captain in 2008 and assigned to work at the Navy Medical Center San Diego. As part of winning the Minerva Award, Pennington was given $25,000 to donate to an organization of her choice. She picked a local organization called the Challenged Athletes Foundation, Operation Rebound, since it works with men and women who have lost a limb in Afghanistan or Iraq. Many of the wounded warriors knew her name; she had taken care of their friends. "It was a sense of closure in a lot of ways. You see such devastation come across your OR table or just come through your unit. Then seeing these men and women preparing for the Beijing Paralympics . . . it was just an amazing, amazing thing. Kind of like a full circle."

Pennington believes that anybody could accomplish what she has done. "You don't have to go to war to be a leader. You don't have to be in the military. . . . Everybody has his or her own combat areas in the world. Every person has their own wars that they have to face whether it's their personal life or at work. It's how you do it that makes a difference," she said.

Common sense was an essential element for this distinguished, humble woman, who claims, "I'm so normal. I'm not brilliant. I wasn't a straight A student. I hate math." She offered, "Don't be afraid to try something different. You always learn. You become an expert, then you do something different and become a novice all over again and work your way up. It still winds up teaching you so many valuable lessons."

Pennington has been able to maintain her individuality while serving in the military. Her personality, her passion for life, and her choice to balance a family with a military profession work with her interests and goals. Most of her bosses when she joined the navy in the mid-eighties did not have children. She has become a role model for others joining now who see by her example that it is possible to have a balance, have children, have it all, and be successful in the military. "When you think of the military, people always think it's these stereotypical women—you're very aggressive or you're very weak. There's no in between. Then they meet you and realize you're just like everybody else. The military is a cross section of the United States. Yet, it is its own little world, and I think that's a great place to be."

She also completed her master's of nursing administration at Old Dominion University. In addition to the Bronze Star, she is the recipient of three Navy Commendation Medals, two Navy Achievement Medals, and the Combat Action Medal.

Pennington deployed to Afghanistan in the summer of 2010 to supervise the care of the critically injured as director of nursing services at the North Atlantic Treaty Organization (NATO) Role 3 Multinational Hospital at Kandahar Air Field. Before leaving she talked with her daughter, who had also decided to become a navy nurse, and assured her that she would be careful not to take added risks to compromise her safety.

9

Rugged War Veteran, Glamorous Single Mom

Master Sgt. Bertha Thompson, USA

Reaching out for help is not weakness. It's actually strength of character
to show that you can confide in someone to seek the necessary help you
need . . . so that you are healthy. You are much stronger for it.

Graduating magna cum laude from her Dallas high school, Bertha "Betty" Thompson had choices. She was offered a four-year college scholarship to attend Southern Methodist University but she turned it down because as a Mexican American she wanted to leave the area where she grew up and go "where there was diversity and everyone was treated equally." She found these values in the army. The military offered a career that promised more than school and work; it provided adventure and travel to interesting places around the world.

Thompson found the adventure she was looking for and more in the U.S. Army. As a seasoned soldier her mental courage and perseverance were tested nearly to the breaking point. She deployed with soldiers to Iraq and Afghanistan as a public affairs professional, supervising a team of army print and broadcast journalists. Members of her team captured live footage of ground combat and dangerous enemy encounters during 2009 that would later be used as stock footage to tell the story of Medal of Honor recipient Staff Sgt. Salvatore Giunta, who risked his life to save a wounded soldier from being captured on the night of October 25, 2007. Giunta became the first living service member from the Iraq or Afghanistan wars to receive the Medal of Honor for his striking gallantry. As proud as she was of her war-tested team of soldiers and her own personal accomplishments as their leader, she was not prepared for the unexpected actions of others. They almost crushed her.

"I didn't want to be an officer," said Thompson. She had enlisted in the army in 1991 at the age of seventeen and attended basic training at Fort Jackson, South Carolina, during her junior year in high school. By the time she graduated from high school in May 1992, she had signed up to attend the three-month advanced training to become a carpentry and masonry specialist at Fort Leonard Wood, Missouri. Under an academic scholarship granted by Texas A&M University, she became a member of the corps of cadets in September and began her officer training. While classes at Texas A&M were ongoing, she deployed with the engineering unit to Belize for their annual two-week training to build schools for villagers in February 1993. Her participation as a reservist and freshman ROTC cadet at the university allowed her to observe and understand the different roles of enlisted and officer service members. By May 1993 she voluntarily returned the three-year army ROTC scholarship and left Texas A&M to pursue a career as an enlisted soldier. The full-tuition, three-year scholarship would have enabled her earn a college degree and immerse herself in courses designed to equip her with the necessary skills and leadership training to become an officer in the army, but she had changed her mind after being a part of the Aggie Corps of Cadets.

Officers tend to have more of a managerial style, looking ahead at the big picture and goals of the unit. Enlisted leaders were hands on, tasked with working directly with the soldiers and completing the daily mission. "I saw how officers and enlisted interacted, and I decided I'd have more of a direct impact with soldiers if I was a noncommissioned officer." She enlisted in the active army in June 1993 and headed to Germany for her first assignment.

These early years of her career were very different and more subdued compared to her later years as a military scribe. Prior to becoming a spokesperson, writer, and international media liaison for the army, she was one of the few enlisted women of her time to become a combat heavy engineer working in construction as a military carpenter. "In 1993 squad leaders were saying, 'I don't want her. Do you want her?'" said Thompson of her superiors. She did not get upset. She knew she was strong and capable. "They didn't know I ran track and cross-country. All they could see was that I was a woman." To the squad leader who took her in, she said, "'You won't regret it.' And he never did."

Thompson honed her skills and leadership style while serving in Vilseck, Germany, with the 94th Engineer Combat Battalion (Heavy), which included a six-month deployment in 1994 with the United Nations Protection Forces in the Republic of Macedonia under Operation Able Sentry. Thompson was one of four females who deployed with three hundred infantrymen assigned to a land brigade, 1–6 Infantry Division. As one of the six unit carpenters, she was assigned to the joint task force Provide Promise, helping improve the quality of life of personnel assigned to the base camp and at other observation posts. These posts were strategically located to monitor military activity near the Macedonian-Serbian-Bulgarian border.

In 1995 she was assigned to the 864th Engineer Combat Battalion (Heavy) at Fort Lewis, Washington. While assigned to the battalion, the soldiers were called upon to help reconstruct airfields, repair roads, build bridges, and fight forest fires. During this period, Thompson earned her rank of sergeant and competed for and won the title 555th Group Soldier of the Quarter. She also received an associate of arts degree from St. Martin's College and married an army engineer.

During a training exercise with that unit, she recalled, an event nearly cost her squad their lives. At Camp Rilea, Oregon, she was training with her squad during a battalion field event using live antitank mines when they armed the top plate with a tilt rod, as instructed by their supervisors, which partially activated the mine. "Thank God we didn't add the fuse," she said. "We would have been blown to pieces." One of the staff sergeants accidentally hit the tilt rod, and it blew up in his face. A piece of shrapnel hit another soldier's leg and cut an artery. The rest of the platoon, protected by the pit, lost their hearing temporarily. Thompson was on top of the steep hill and called for immediate medical evacuation. "It took a five-ton truc k to get them both out since the ambulance could not make it down the hill." Both of the men barely survived, but they were "never the same." The truck drove to an open football field, where a helicopter evacuated them to the nearest hospital. Later the investigation revealed that the tilt rods were not an authorized part of this training.

During her deployment with Able Sentry, a photojournalist snapped a picture of her laying the foundation for a chapel. Seeing the power of the moment preserved in that image, she decided to pursue journalism. It rekindled her passion from high school, when she had been the newspaper editor for four years. She had not known the army had photojournalists and appreciated the opportunity to illuminate the army's stories for the press and the public. Her first journalism assignment sent her to Fort Leonard Wood, Missouri, where she became the Training and Doctrine Command Military Journalist of the Year in 1998 and earned her bachelor of science in English from Drury University. She worked as an assistant editor of the Fort Leonard Wood *Guidon* (formerly *Essayons*), a post newspaper. Then, she opted to return overseas as the non commissioned officer in charge of the Europe Regional Medical Command Public Affairs Office in Heidelberg, Germany, from 1999 to 2003. During this assignment, she gave birth to her daughter, Laura, at the Heidelberg Hospital.

Thompson's leadership and management skills continued to advance, and they were noted and praised. She was selected to become a senior drill sergeant and served from 2003 to 2005 at Fort George G. Meade, Maryland, while completing her master of education degree from the University of Oklahoma. She appreciated every minute those days provided to shape civilians into future soldiers and leaders. "We did so much, slept very little, and kept going on fumes." During deployment later on, she ran into some of these young soldiers. "Most of them thanked me for my 'tough love' leadership style."

Thompson deployed to combat zones twice and helped manage the demand from international media to be in the field with the troops during engagements in Iraq and Afghanistan. She volunteered for these positions even though she was a single mom and would have to leave her daughter for the dangers of war. Her first deployment was in support of Operation Iraqi Freedom with a Public Affairs Operations Center in 2006. Owing to a shortage of officers to help with media, she worked directly with then Lt. Col. Christopher Garver, commander of the Tenth Public Affairs Operation Center, headquartered at Fort McPherson, Georgia. He assigned her to the Media Operations Center at the U.S. Embassy in Baghdad, where she was positioned to assist as a press officer and spokesperson for the generals.

Her second combat deployment was in 2009, when she was the first sergeant of the Fifth Mobile Public Affairs Detachment (MPAD) supporting Operation Enduring Freedom in Bagram, Afghanistan, with smaller teams at Forward Operating Base (FOB) Fenty, FOB Salerno, and FOB Shank. She supported the brigade combat teams while the rest of the unit operated the media support center in Bagram. She was given ten months to turn around from her Iraqi deployment and prepare a team to deploy for this assignment. Part of the preparation was going to Hohenfels, Germany, with the 3-2 Stryker Brigade out of Fort Lewis, Washington, for a training exercise dubbed Cooperative Spirit 2008. Her unit's mission was to run the Combined Press Information Center, to provide electronic newsgathering, and to escort embedded media while the troops exercised in a simulated Afghanistan-like environment. The 3-2 Stryker Brigade supplied support to participating Australian, British, Canadian, and New Zealand armies. Thompson and her team moved with the soldiers, escorting the press while documenting the exercise battlefield with photos and video. The exercises resembled the missions in Iraq and Afghanistan, like clearing buildings and doing security patrols, with print and broadcast journalists closely following the soldiers around corners into unpredictable environments—including live fire. These preparations provided a glimpse of the Afghanistan war environment and the type of battle mind-set it required.

After Germany, Thompson returned with her team to Fort Lewis until they left for Afghanistan. Then the real mission began. Her detachment of less than twenty was broken down into teams of three led by junior sergeants. Army journalists wrote stories, took photos, and gathered video of the troops performing their duties. The army public affairs specialists would assist the media with their newsgathering by guiding them and coordinating their needs with the priorities of the combat missions.

Thompson's team started with the 101st Airborne Division from Fort Campbell, Kentucky, and completed the deployment with the 82nd Airborne Division from Fort Bragg, North Carolina. Her team served as media escorts and as embedded military journalists with the various brigade combat teams, following missions that provided security, governance, and reconstruction. Sometimes, as with the Medal of Honor recipient's story, it involved being in the right place at the right time to record stock footage which would later be used to re-create a portion of the heroic battle taking place as Giunta moved in to save his fellow soldier. "Staff Sgt. Justin Puetz took the footage of them running up the hill. Then you hear the firefight. There was an explosion nearby. He didn't even turn away or move the camera," said Thompson proudly of her subordinate's efforts. CBS's *60 Minutes* ran their story using the footage provided by the army.

Another one of her public affairs soldiers, Staff Sgt. Matthew Moeller, took many great photos documenting the work of the soldiers. It was a tough job and one in which they encountered harsh situations. "They [Moeller and the light infantry squad of army soldiers] went through the Korengal Valley. Nothing happened that they didn't anticipate. It was just that they were trekking through a pretty dangerous place with probably the worst conditions in Afghanistan," said Thompson. "We fostered relationships with the units—we have lifelong relationships because of it." Moeller was named the SSG Paul D. Savanuck Military Print Journalist of the Year in 2009 and later earned a spot as one of two army journalists attending a one-year photojournalism program at Syracuse University.

Thompson also went out in the field for battlefield circulation, which involved going outside the wire for three weeks at a time. "I'd rather be in the fight than behind the desk," she said. Thompson understood being an effective leader was not pushing paper but knowing the environment and having an acute awareness of her team's needs. When she preplanned her trips, she asked her subordinates to pick the places to go—even if it was dangerous—and that's where they went. Looking out for her team's welfare, equipment, and climate needs—like issues to be resolved or giving clarification for command decisions, mentoring, and sometimes being a disciplinarian—were an inherent part of the "circulation." She would have gone out more, but couldn't because she was also responsible for the administrative needs of her unit and providing updates to the unit commander. As soon as a member returned to the United States, Thompson filled the vacancy to augment and circulate in the field again. "I felt a deep need to be with my soldiers who were in the action and in the fight. I would not make a soldier do anything that I would not expect from myself." Equally important, she wisely went out to meet the unit leadership that her teams supported and to establish relationships that would be beneficial to her soldiers in the field. "I would make it easier for them to maneuver around."

The stress of the war's environment was amped up when a barrage of mortars and bombs were aimed at the U.S. Embassy in Baghdad. "You can run to a bunker, but most of the time when the bombings happen you're sleeping. It was at those times when I just laid in my bed and put my hands together and prayed."

There were also times when Thompson joined the teams and soldiers on patrol. With the 2-12 Infantry, she patrolled outside FOB Blessing, a small base located in a valley of Kunar Province that was frequently under insurgent fire. "The day I showed up and went out with them they said, 'It never rains and it's raining today. We usually get shot at and we're not. It must be you. You're our lucky charm.'" The command was also impressed with her leadership. She explained to the senior enlisted representative what her team's mission was and said if there were any issues to contact her for assistance. By offering her help she was a resource for the command and enabled her team to embed as a valuable resource rather than be perceived as a hindrance. This made a difference in a war-torn environment where every day the unexpected should be expected.

One of Thompson's favorite memories of going out on patrol was meeting with leaders from a local town during a *shura*, or tribal consultation. After the meeting, she was shown one of the schools, and the infantry leaders invited her to sit down and talk with them. "The leader looked me in the eye and shook my hand, knowing I was a woman. I appreciated that he was acknowledging me as a female leader. To me it was important." Shuras are a traditional meeting where people from the local area can discuss topics important to their livelihood. They are similar to a town council meeting except the male rulers of the Muslim tribe did not allow Afghan women to attend the shura. "The more we know about people the better. We can learn to accept the differences. That's why I joined the army. I wanted to know more than my culture—the Mexican American culture. I wanted to understand multicultures."

Thompson was able to understand the battlefield, the Afghanistan culture, and the soldiers in the field. She was ready for the dangers of the war. "I was prepared psychologically to deal with that. I knew I could possibly die. I did a glamour photo session with my daughter a year in advance of the deployment knowing what could happen." She recognized she could be maimed, her face or body changed forever, and she was ready for that. She also knew that she could come back "different" because of the things she would see and experience dealing with the enemy. She was prepared for that as well.

What she was not prepared for was when people she trusted in the army would cross boundaries of respect. "As a senior drill sergeant, I was accustomed to having soldiers come to me with very personal, private matters. You open up to your leaders expecting a certain amount of confidentiality and trust. You never expect a breach of that trust." She trusted two of her leaders, shared a lot about her personal story, and sought their advice. What started out as admiration and respect for their role as leaders and mentors turned into a dire situation for her when they made inappropriate comments of a sexual nature. "Then it became physical," she said. "I'm shaking a hand and the hand pulls me toward him. I caught myself, when the toes of my boots were barely touching the ground. I quickly pushed back and pulled away. Thankfully I never allowed it to go any further. Then for a long time I beat myself up thinking, *Where did I go wrong? Did I send out the wrong message?* I think they had me questioning myself, and I didn't do anything."

Thompson struggled with facing the reality that a sexual harassment situation was surrounding her professionally and tormenting her mentally. "It took me a long time to admit to myself that this was taking place." Her situation was especially difficult because she was deployed to Afghanistan on a restricted base targeted daily by insurgents and she and her harassers were working in a close space. She still had to make leadership decisions and seek day-to-day counsel with both of the senior male noncommissioned officers in her chain of command who were acting out of line.

She stopped running for exercise and stress release and instead tried to avoid the precarious situation she was embroiled in. "A lot of times I just endured certain things they said and suffered in silence. When I could not take it anymore, I had to say something. I had to report it."

Thompson knew that what she disclosed to the command about the sexual harassment mattered. It's on record and the offenders are on notice. She does not regret taking action and believes that what she did will prevent it from happening again to someone else. "If you do say something it marks you. If you don't say anything it still hurts you. What I would tell other women in a similar situation—do what you feel is right in your heart and do what you can afford to deal with in the future as a result."

Even though she was "marked," or labeled a whistle blower, professionally for bringing the situation out into the open and holding accountable the senior enlisted leaders for their illegal and unacceptable actions, she found support from some. Other colleagues withdrew from Thompson because they were afraid of retribution; the harassers were also supervising them and the situation became a "battle of ethics." Thompson said, "It felt like I was dealing with the playground bullies in first grade. Back then I could beat them up; I won."

She learned from her experience that jobs are changeable. How you feel inside is something that you'll have to be able to live with. She also discovered by speaking out that there was a community of people from all ranks and walks of life who came forward and surrounded her with support. The same community a year later still called her to ask her how she was doing. "I wouldn't say I was devastated because it didn't completely destroy me. But I would say that a part of me changed after I left Afghanistan." When she returned to the United States she knew she needed to move on and that it would take time. "The person who got to see me in that phase was my daughter, Laura." From the time Thompson picked up her daughter after the deployment in February to May 2010, then nine-year-old Laura witnessed her mother overcome with emotion stemming from the impression the experiences in Afghanistan had made. They were resurfacing as she tried to process the trauma and instead became depressed.

Working through her pain was especially tough because Thompson was single. She had divorced in 2006, right before she had gone to Iraq, and her daughter was living with the father, who also served in the army. "We both love her very much." It was the one thing they agreed on. When Laura's father had to turn over custody a month before Thompson returned from Iraq, Laura stayed with Thompson's parents and remained there until February 2010. In order to provide stability for her daughter, Thompson decided that Laura should continue to stay with her grandparents. This enabled Thompson to again undergo the intense pre-deployment training and prepare for her 2009 deployment to Afghanistan. It also allowed her ex-husband an opportunity to deploy to Afghanistan. "Every year just kept passing and next thing you know it's been four years," said Thompson.

At the time of the interview, mother and daughter had lived together in New York for a year. "We recently made pudding. To me that's the best thing ever, watching her make it. I enjoy hearing her play the clarinet, wrong notes and all. She's also the one that watched me cry when I came back."

Thompson received her annual evaluation in New York, where she's been assigned since returning from the war zone serving as the noncommissioned officer in charge of Army Public Affairs Northeast. With top marks and a recommendation for promotion to sergeant major she was up for selection to command sergeant major. Thompson has enjoyed her work in New York City, managing the office and interacting with top-tier media. When Bobbi Brown, makeup artist to the stars, wanted to pamper a female soldier for a holiday makeover on NBC's *Today Show* in 2010, Thompson was honored to be selected and was joined by her daughter on the program.

Thompson had a hard time during her first months back in America because she was remembering Afghanistan and her demeaning experience. "But it didn't stop there. What happened, at the same time, was . . . you know how you have personality conflicts? I had some difficulties with the boss. I tried to address them in a nice way but with some people you can't. It makes it worse. That's how I ended up going for help with these other two. Rather than helping me they crossed the line. That's too much for one person, don't you think? Three against one."

She was baffled and to this day is confused by her female former boss and the "personality conflict" between them. The boss gave Thompson a poor evaluation that she planned to appeal. "I have sisters. I know each one has a different experience and has to deal with things in their own way. This is especially true for women in the military. But not all women are open to talking with another woman. Some women can be your worst enemy." Thompson would have preferred having the option to go to a network of women when something like this happened. For her, the compounding situation was nearly overwhelming and emotionally consuming. She was embarrassed. "It was like, how can you explain this? You can't. It was all about boundaries, people respecting each other. Because they are senior, sometimes people forget they [subordinates] are human beings. You still have to respect others."

Over the past year she's been finding ways to heal. First, she had to admit to herself she was having difficulty. "I think the thing that finally did it for me was Gen. Carter Ham's story. He came out and said that after he returned from Iraq—where some of his soldiers were killed during a dining facility bombing—he was having difficulties reconciling what had happened there. He knew something was wrong. His wife knew something was wrong. He decided to get help." Thompson thought Ham was a fantastic leader; she had served under his command the first time she deployed with Task Force Able Sentry to Macedonia in 1994. After hearing his story, she decided to get help by talking with military women and spending time with her mother. "It's not weakness," she said. "It's actually strength of character to show you can confide in someone to seek the necessary help you need to get past it so that you are healthy. You are much stronger for it."

Thompson definitely learned a lot and was strong enough to share her story to benefit others. Her passion for running has come back again. During her cross-country move to New York, the work she started on the appeal of her performance evaluation had begun to engross her. When she realized her daughter was not getting her time or attention—Laura was sitting at home instead of playing in the pool because Thompson was working on the appeal—she boxed it up and let it go. "When I look at the appeal and my evaluation, it's really not that big a deal a year later. Plus, I've met someone and we're having a baby. I think I'll retire. If I change my mind I can do that and still be competitive for promotion."

Thompson is keeping her options open and leaning toward studying law with her post 9/11 GI Bill benefits in part inspired by her own tribulations and desire to empower people. "I want to be able to start a nonprofit to help soldiers who go through trauma," she said. "I've met so many people who are suffering that I want to offer them a recovery room or place where they can laugh and get their mind off the bad stuff."

10

From Colorado to Congress

Rep. Heather A. Wilson, USAF (Ret.)

Stay in school is the first thing I would advise young people today.
Then find a dream—a dream that's bigger than you. Not society's
dream for who you should be but your own very personal dream of who
you are and who you would like to become. If you pursue that dream,
then work isn't work and your life has tremendous satisfaction.
It doesn't matter what the dream is—it just matters that it's your dream.

The first woman U.S. armed service veteran to serve in Congress was Rep. Heather A. Wilson. A U.S. Air Force Academy graduate, Rhodes Scholar, and former National Security Council staff member, she was sworn into the House in 1998.

Wilson became the second woman to represent New Mexico and the first Republican woman elected in that state. She had campaigned with the slogan, "Fighting for our families." Her agenda sought better public schools and the elimination of the marriage penalty and estate taxes. Wilson prevailed against millionaire Democratic state senator Phillip Maloof. After winning her House seat, she received assignments on the Energy and Commerce Committee and the subcommittees Telecommunication, Energy and Air Quality, and Environmental and Hazardous Materials for the duration of her House career, which ended in 2009. She was also on the Permanent Select Committee on Intelligence, which she left in 2001 for the powerful Armed Services Committee. With two installations in her district, Kirtland Air Force Base and the

Sandia National Laboratories, Wilson had a prime vantage point to oversee concerns. Two years later, she left the Armed Services Committee to return to the Intelligence Committee and chair the Subcommittee on Technical and Tactical Intelligence.

Wilson was not reluctant to take positions independent of her party. She called for tax code simplification and criticized the North Atlantic Treaty Organization bombing of Kosovo in 1999. On social issues she supported requiring that health plans for federal workers include contraceptive coverage and voted down an amendment that would have banned adoptions by gay parents in the District of Columbia. In 2006 she was a leader in efforts to provide congressional oversight of the president's terrorist surveillance program.

"I think the most satisfying thing about being a member of Congress is constituent service," said Wilson. "It's the basics that do not usually get public attention." Wilson enjoyed working with people and especially liked to help those who came into her office irate with the way the federal government mishandled something. Once a woman walked into her office upset that Social Security had stopped sending her checks. The reason? They said she was dead. "Well, she was looking pretty lively to me," Wilson recalled. "Untangling problems like that, assisting a dad who had trouble getting into the VA hospital, or helping when immigration paperwork is messed up for a child are things that are personally satisfying to me." Wilson believed it was important for her to relate to her constituents by communicating with them, talking about their life and their needs. She reached out to those who came to her for help with problems by making them feel at ease. "Most of my constituents probably don't know that I have a doctoral degree. They don't know what a Rhodes Scholarship is, and they don't care," she shared. "What they are concerned about is that they have a representative who wants to help them. I'm someone who understands the problems they face in life—I think that's more important than my education."

Public service was a natural calling for Wilson who was born in Fitzwilliam, New Hampshire, in 1960. When her father, a U.S. Air Force veteran, died after her second grade school year, the family moved and she grew up in Keene, New Hampshire. Her mother, a nurse, and her father taught their children to pitch in, give back to their community, and show respect for their country. Politics was not necessarily part of dinnertime conversation. A sense of patriotism and respect for their community were part of their way of life. "I can tell you that if my brothers and I did not get our butts off the sidewalk during the Memorial Day parade when the flag came by, we were going to be dragged up by the scruff of our necks," she said.

"Probably more than any other single event, the tragedy of my father's death changed the course of my life," said Wilson. "My dad wasn't there. I was probably much more independent and stronger because of this loss. I also had a sense of life's impermanence, that you'd better seize today. It's not necessarily a long life, so you make every day count."

Her mother later remarried. During Wilson's middle and high school years, the family dealt with another troubling period. Her stepfather, a police officer, was an alcoholic. He had lost his job too. "Everybody faces challenges in life. I think I have a certain empathy for people who are facing tough times."

School became a refuge for her. She felt successful there. It was a place where she excelled and received tremendous satisfaction from the curriculum, which she found interesting. College was something she was determined to pursue, even though no one in her family had ever gone to college. She applied to several universities and the U.S. Air Force Academy in Colorado Springs, Colorado. The military academy offered her a full scholarship. "Certainly the tuition at the academy was attractive," she laughed. But it also offered an invitation to the world. Growing up in a small town she knew there were doctors, nurses, lawyers, and other professional possibilities for meaningful work, but she had an idea that there were other careers in which she could achieve success. Her father and grandfather had inspired her global thinking because of the way they led their lives.

Wilson's grandfather, fondly known as Scotty, flew in the Royal Air Force during World War I. In 1922, he came to America from Scotland and worked as a barnstormer, offering sightseeing flights in aircraft made of wood and fabric. He pursued his American dream by opening little airports across New England. The family's connection to aviation was very strong and was passed from generation to generation. Wilson's father started flying when he was thirteen years old and got his pilot's license when he turned sixteen. He was a pilot for the air force at the time when jet engines were the latest leap forward. He continued to fly throughout his life.

The smell of jet fuel and the experience of flying and hanging out at airports still trigger for Wilson fond memories of her childhood with her dad. Even after her father's death, his flying buddies would take her up to explore the skies and see the landscape from above. The legacy of military service her father and grandfather bequeathed to her was influential. It was natural for her to want to be in aviation. She thought about being an experimental test pilot. It would be fun. Going to the academy was her first step out into the world beyond her rural town in pursuit of her dream to fly.

"When I went to the Air Force Academy [1978–1982] the F-16 fighter was the newest thing," said Wilson. The education she received at the academy was extraordinary, even though some barriers still existed for the women cadets, who were only recently admitted to the academy. Since 1954, when President Dwight D. Eisenhower signed a bill establishing the U.S. Air Force Academy, it had always been a university for men. According to the academy's own website, "perhaps the most controversial event in academy history was the admission of women." The first women permitted to enter the nation's military academies graduated in 1980. Wilson said, "The Class of 1980 had kind of broken the initial barrier. In some ways I think it might have been easier for the first four or five classes than it was in the 1990s. By the 1990s the leadership at the academy was determined to make it work." The leadership was refreshed and helped oversee the sluggish organizational and cultural change of an all-male environment to one that incorporated women.

Of the 4,000 cadets in the entire student body in the late 1970s, there were about 840 women, or 21 percent. The everyday requirements and pressure to excel were intense for everyone. The challenging academics, exercises in learning how to be a military officer, and physical fitness requirements all made for a taxing and busy day. There was also added scrutiny of the women from the media and public, who were interested in how this historic change was going. "If things got off track someone noticed pretty quickly. That said, there were people there who didn't think we belonged." This unwelcoming undertone added another responsibility for the young women cadets. "They had to try and change the attitudes of their peers and also of the officer corps senior to them," Wilson recalled.

Entering the Air Force Academy two years after the admissions barrier was lifted did not mean the cultural barriers had dissipated and that the males accepted female officers as future leaders. Many of the male officers had entered the air force at a time when the women they served with (if any) were severely limited in what they were allowed to do. Career fields for women were very narrow before the mid-1970s—restricted to administration, nursing, and the like. The first women to go through pilot training went between 1976 and 1977. Women were also not allowed promotions above the rank of lieutenant colonel, and they could be no more than 2 percent of the force. This was a stark contrast to the opportunities open to men, for whom the sky was the limit. "So a lot of senior officers at the academy had not served with women as peers or subordinates, let alone as their supervisors. There were times that became an issue," she said.

Sometimes the issue was seemingly playful in nature. "As a freshman, everybody gets hassled, which is part of the initiation and military indoctrination at service academies." One day while she was "calling minutes"—standing below a clock in the barracks and announcing in a loud voice the time remaining before the noon meal gathering of cadets—Wilson experienced this from a fellow cadet. She said she has always had an unusually low voice, which was particularly apparent during her announcements in the corridor. As the squadron marched out for formation she was instructed to remind them as the clock ticked, "Sir, there are now fifteen minutes before the noon meal formation. The uniform of the day is. . . . The menu for lunch is. . . ." In the process of doing her job, an upperclassman walked by and made a sexist, derogatory comment about her voice. One of his classmates, a woman in the Class of 1981, overheard and called him on it. She ordered him to knock it off, saying in effect, "'We don't do that here!' I thought that from then on she was a hero."

Other times the hassling could be more serious and harmful. As a senior, because she excelled academically and in military bearing, Wilson was selected from among the thousand members of the upper class to become the commander of the wing, or top-ranking cadet. Because it was the dead of winter, Wilson chose to wear trousers to the interview, although skirts were also an option. The interviewing officer, a colonel with twenty years in the service, had recently been assigned to the academy. He did not know Wilson. "Some of the questions he asked during that interview I would not tolerate now," she explained. "It was clear to me by the end of the interview that there wasn't a snowball's chance in hell that he was going to choose me for that job."

She recalled that his first question to her was if she had any objections to wearing skirts, followed by a bunch of questions about what women think. When it came to explaining her leadership style she said she was fairly participative in getting people to buy into decisions. "I remember he said, 'Well, what I really mean is when it comes right down to it, how can you give an order to a guy?' I'm there to be a commander of a 4,000-person organization as a cadet, and he kept asking me those kinds of questions. At the time I'm twenty years old. I'm trying to make it through the academy, and I'm doing exceptionally well. I was also applying for the Rhodes. If I had more maturity and experience I probably would have called him on it, saying, 'Sir, that's an inappropriate question and you know it is.'"

The experience did cause Wilson later in life, as a woman in a position of authority and power, to have an obligation to take action when something similar happened to someone else. "I can do that now in ways that I could not when I was twenty," she shared. "I just described to you two instances that were five minutes out of a four-year career. I also built wonderful friendships there. I got a fantastic education and am deeply grateful for my experience at the academy. I was mentored by some wonderful people, mostly men, because there weren't many women officers. My mentors saw potential in me and sought to develop that promise."

Wilson's talent and capability was indeed great. Before graduating from the academy, she applied for and was selected as one of the Rhodes Scholars representing the United States. Women were allowed to apply in 1976. Wilson was the second female Rhodes Scholar to graduate from the U.S. Air Force Academy. Of the thirty-six Scholars from the academy so far, five have been women.

The American contingent of thirty-two students joined other scholars from around the world at England's University of Oxford, one of the world's most ancient and distinguished universities. According to an Oxford/Rhodes brochure, scholars are selected for their potential over a lifetime for "excellence in qualities of mind and in qualities of person, which in combination, offer the promise of effective service to the world in the decades ahead."

Wilson flew across the Atlantic to reside in England for two years. The Oxford learning experience was quite different from her last four years in college. At the academy learning was so intense that it "felt like I was trying to drink from a fire hydrant. At Oxford, it was the reverse of that. It was as if you walked into a treasure room and they said, 'Take anything you want, but you can only have what you can carry.'" So the difficult choice for Wilson was to choose how to spend her time and how to absorb from "wonderful libraries, instructors, and professors." She chose to immerse herself in the study of international relations, learning in depth about twentieth-century history and international politics.

Upon leaving the university in 1985, she had earned a master's and a doctorate in international relations. The air force assigned her to U.S. Air Force headquarters in England to assist with international concerns. Next stop was Brussels, Belgium, where she assisted during the initial talks for the Treaty on Conventional Armed Forces in Europe. She was briefly assigned to serve in Vienna, Austria, during the beginning of negotiations for the treaty, which was based on the participating countries' desire to create an environment of stability and structure for military force development in Europe. At the time, Reagan's presidency and the Cold War were coming to an end. Twenty-three nations, members of the NATO and Warsaw Pact, sought to improve relations with the Soviet Union and allow for Soviet troop withdrawal in a transparent way during what could have been a very tumultuous time. In dramatic meetings with Soviet leader Mikhail Gorbachev, Reagan negotiated a treaty that would eliminate intermediate-range nuclear missiles and establish parity as well as transparency and stability in the balance of conventional military forces in Europe.

President George H. W. Bush entered the White House in 1989. Wilson, now a captain in the air force, had completed her obligated service. She left the military to join the National Security Council staff as director for European Defense Policy and Arms Control. Her principal responsibility was stewarding the treaty to completion. This meant facilitating and forwarding guidance from the Defense Department, Joint Chiefs of Staff, State Department, and others to the ambassador negotiating the treaty. "You have to get everybody on the same page regarding the parameters of what the American negotiation position should be at what is an arms control conference," Wilson shared. "Having worked overseas before I worked in Washington, I learned that it's a whole lot harder to get the State Department and the Defense Department to agree than it is to get the Americans and the Soviets to agree."

The morning the Berlin Wall fell in Germany she walked down to the office of the director for European and Soviet Affairs. "He was sitting in one of these Queen Anne chairs with high wings and had his hand resting up by his face watching the televised event of the fall of the wall. It occurred to me that what everybody was watching as an event in history, and we—the White House and the president—had to decide what to do about it." President Bush made the decision to help push for reunification of Germany over objections from the French and British. "That was a pivotal decision in the history of Europe."

Choosing not to seek reelection to a sixth term in the House, she instead ran in 2008 for an open U.S. Senate seat being vacated by New Mexico senator Pete Domenici. Wilson narrowly lost the Republican primary. At the conclusion of the 110th Congress, the married mother of three retired from the House on January 3, 2009. She and her husband live in Albuquerque with their two teenagers.

On March 7, 2011, she announced her candidacy for U.S. Senate in New Mexico.

11

In the Men's House: Class of 1980

Sharon (Hanley) Disher, U.S. Naval Academy; Marene (Nyberg) Allison, U.S. Military Academy; Capt. Sue (Donner) Bibeau (Ret.), U.S. Coast Guard Academy; and Brig. Gen. Paula G. Thornhill (Ret.), U.S. Air Force Academy

The idea that there needs to be inclusionary leadership is one we're still maturing into. Control and authority can be shared without the threat existing between people who are very different from each other. When you're talking about organizational change, thirty years is not that long.

—Capt. Sue Bibeau, USCG (Ret.)
former director of admissions for the U.S. Coast Guard Academy

The 1976 high school graduation season marked the beginning of a ground-breaking and shocking journey for the 395 women entering the first coeducational class at America's prestigious military service academies. Before they arrived at their respective academies, their anticipated arrivals were resisted and fought by armed forces leaders, academy leadership, faculty members, and male cadets. The women were viewed as intruders. People reacted as if a dust-carrying windstorm had arrived and needed to be shut out, but with the passage of legislation in 1975 signed by President Gerald R. Ford, Congress ordered the military service academies to open their doors to women.* The law broke with tradition and shook the foundations of each academy's collegial core and created a friction that sparked persistent questions: Why would women choose to live in traditionally all-male barracks, marching, studying,

---

* The United States Merchant Marine Academy accepted women in 1974. Graduates of USMMA were commissioned reserve officers unlike those of the DOD service academies and the USCGA who immediately served as officers on active duty.

and learning to be military officers when U.S. law prohibited them from combat roles? Why should a woman take the place of a man who could serve in combat? Do women really belong at military service academies? Why is a woman taking my son's place at the academy?

For the nation's oldest service academy, West Point, the struggle included adjusting to a 174-year policy change. More importantly, changing the law did not change the culture for those of the "Long Gray Line" or at any of the other service academies. The Air Force Academy, the newest of the service academies, from 1964 to 2004 displayed the inscribed words "Bring me men . . . " at the base of a ramp where new cadets arrived to start their transition into the military. Apparently it would take decades for organizational change.

Those who did not support this coed initiative failed to foresee that accepting women would produce long-term benefits for each service and lead to the successful, innovative careers of women officers and the integration of women in the military, enabling a sustained volunteer force ready to fight wars on multiple fronts. For the women cadets, who were merely seventeen or eighteen years old, it was a four-year journey of survival, struggle, and exclusion. Naturally, they did not have a built-in support structure even among themselves at the schools. The women would bear the harshness of this burden, and their lives would be forever changed by their bravery and solidarity.

For the women who joined the Class of 1980 at a military service academy, the opportunity seemed exciting. They saw their futures filled with adventure. They would serve their country unlike ever before. They could earn the equivalent of an Ivy League education and learn to be combat leaders. They would be commissioned officers. All in all, they would have an unforgettable and inconceivable experience. Interviewed thirty-one years later, here are the stories of four of these women.

III

The few weeks between high school graduation and the July 6, 1976, Induction Day passed quickly for Sharon (Hanley) Disher, who lived in Portsmouth, New Hampshire. She was going to the Naval Academy in Annapolis, Maryland. Encouraged by her father, a career air force pilot, she had accepted her appointment knowing that it would be a way to serve in the military and become a pilot, her ultimate goal. She had enjoyed the opportunities to travel her family had been given while her father came up through the ranks as an enlisted corpsman in the navy and later saw him join the pilot program. "To be honest, I was clueless about what an academy was or the rigor that was there. I knew it would be a challenge, and that was appealing," said Disher.

Disher's friends thought she was inspirational. For the most part, her teachers and others who knew her were excited for her. Some of the high school parents, though, were not. There was a moment before she left home that may seem silly but was an important factor to how she endured the next four years at the academy. Disher played the flute in the high school band with a girl named Patty Labell. One day Labell came to practice loudly exclaiming, "'My mother said you'll never make it because you're too much of a party girl.'" Disher said that Mrs. Labell's comment got her through the Naval Academy because "I was going to show her that I could."

Starting with Induction Day, there were tougher challenges ahead for Disher, one of the eighty-one first women to attend Annapolis. The seniors, first class midshipmen, were polite and almost cool during the dawn of the day. They helped Disher and her classmates get checked in and took them around to get gear, vaccination shots, and room assignments. They taught them the "five basic responses" they were to use in answering questions and how to wear the uniform, salute, and march in preparation for the Induction Ceremony that night at six o'clock. Before dusk, the good-bye march for parents and friends began for those who would not see them again until they completed the two-month-long rite of passage. "Everybody's weepy and nervous and scared. We were exhausted from the day and sweaty because there was no air-conditioning and it was 95 degrees with 95 percent humidity," remembered Disher. She quickly said good-bye to her parents before returning to begin the heated initiation. "My mother's last words to me were, 'You can come home anytime. You can call me and I will be right there,' because I think she understood what being the first meant. I had no idea." Years later she would discover a secret her mother had kept—for the next two weeks her mother never left the house and listened for the phone.

After the ceremony, twelve hundred men and women of the Class of 1980 squared their corners and scurried like frightened rats into the wardroom, the officer's mess, for dinner where everyone ate meals at the same time while seated twelve to a table. At the head of the table where Disher sat were two seniors. One was a platoon leader and the other a squad leader of nine plebes, or freshmen. Disher and her classmates were instructed to take the serving trays heaping with the evening meal and pass them to the head of the table. As was tradition, the plebes were the last to be served and last to eat. "We were all scared and they're yelling at us because we're not getting the food to them fast enough," said Disher of the surf-and-turf menu of steak and lobster. The tension and stress were overwhelming. She was not able to eat and just wanted to leave the table. Forgetting how to ask properly by sticking her arm straight out and making a fist while keeping her "eyes in the boat," or staring straight ahead, she simply asked to be excused. It was a mistake. She had not waited to be called upon. Her platoon leader went around the table asking if any of her classmates knew how to ask properly to be excused. No one did. She was off that particular hook, but in the next moment, stuck on a much larger one. He stood up and put his knuckles on the table, wrinkling the linen tablecloth. Leaning over he pointed his finger at her and shouted with intensity, "Miss Hanley, I don't like women in my school. I don't want women in my school. It will be my mission for the next year to make sure you are gone before I graduate. Is that clear?" She wondered which of her five basic responses she could use for that question. "It was another real defining moment for me," said Disher. "I thought, *You don't think I can make it here? You are wrong. I'm going to make it here just because of you.*"

Disher and her classmates had been blind to what they were up against. "In high school we were the leaders. We were class president or yearbook editor, and no one questioned us being in leadership positions because we were girls. Then we went to the academy and everything we did was wrong because we were girls." *Where did this come from?* she wondered.

Trying to understand was not an option. Who had the time? Her platoon leader had selected a room next to hers and made every waking moment difficult for Disher and her two female roommates. She describes in detail the climate, environment, and some of the struggles she and other women experienced and witnessed as midshipmen at the Naval Academy in her 1998 book, *First Class: Women Join the Ranks at the Naval Academy.* "I was very gentle when talking about the academy in my book," said Disher. "It's really the tip of the iceberg."

III

When Marene (Nyberg) Allison accepted the appointment to West Point, her parents were supportive. "Nobody said, 'This is going to be horrendous. You're in the first class with women and it's going to be awful,'" said Allison. "The academy was absolutely unprepared for women to arrive." Lt. Gen. Sidney B. Berry, the superintendent who was in the midst of sorting out one of the most serious cheating scandals in West Point's history, informed the graduating class of 1976 that he was extremely opposed to women entering West Point, said Allison. Weeks later, one hundred and nineteen women joined the freshman class at West Point on July 7, 1976.

The West Point leaders reacted with a strict interpretation of the law, creating a climate that was not prepared for women because they did not think women should be there. Women were included in training with male cadets—rising at reveille, 6:10 a.m.; attending classes from 7:50 a.m. until 11:55 a.m.; and continuing on through the day at an exhausting pace until taps at 11 p.m.

The academy administration may have believed they had adequately prepared for the first coeducational class, but according to Allison, they had not. The obvious necessary logistical arrangements had been made, such as converting a few men's latrines, or bathrooms, into women's rooms, but ironically, the presence of women was not given much thought in other important ways. For example, the women were issued men's shirts and boots, which did not fit well, were not tailored or attractive, and were not something they could wear proudly. They were also issued gray full dress coats without tails, under the assumption that such coats would not accentuate a women's behind, said Allison. Moreover, not much thought had been given to the fact that when cadets actually wore the coat over white pants, the white behinds would be much more obvious without coattails, especially when women were first classmen and moved to the rear of the formation. The women looked out of place.

The gray pants were women's sizes but had fragile plastic zippers that broke within the first twenty-four hours or so of being worn, so safety pins had to be used to hold them up. The men's pants had metal zippers. "They issued you men's pajamas with that nice little opening down below," Allison said cynically. "The bathrobes they gave us were so short, and I am tall. I just thought, *Could I expose any more of my body to you [male peers]?*"

The lack of thoughtfulness given to uniforms designed for women carried over to the preparation of the men to accept women as equal but diverse members of the Corps of Cadets. Allison recalled that after the initial short haircuts given to all the freshmen plebes, her platoon sergeant insisted that she continue to have her hair cut as short as the men. Her hair was less than an inch long for weeks. Her tactical officer, the officer who oversaw how the senior cadets managed each company, asked her why she kept getting her hair cut. He gave her a direct order to stop after she explained the situation. "Telling me but not telling my platoon sergeant, where does that put me?" Allison added, "Not good." She kept getting haircuts as directed by her immediate supervisor.

III

"I think in a lot of ways I was very naïve," said Sue (Donner) Bibeau of her acceptance of her Coast Guard Academy appointment. "All of us (the women in my class) had been brought up post-1960s and came in with the same kind of framework. Opportunities for women were expanding dramatically. Probably for the first time in our country's history women would have the opportunity to do whatever they wanted. The novelty and potential risks of going to a service academy were not on my mind."

What was on her mind was the sense of adventure, a prominent career serving her country, and the excitement of being a part of the U.S. Coast Guard's missions. Going to an academy, with its full four-year scholarship, also seemed to be a good way to finance her college education.

She learned of the Coast Guard Academy through a mailing that came to her house in a suburb of Springfield, Massachusetts. "It was certainly not a decision supported by my high school guidance counselors," she said. "There was a certain premium put on kids in my high school going to an Ivy League school or first-tier college primarily in New England. I was disappointing to them, I suppose. That's okay." It was also an unusual move for a female in her community to go to a service academy. Although her friends thought it was fine and her parents supported her, many adults were not so sure.

Bibeau was more concerned about the physical demands and tests she would have to pass to enter and remain at the academy than what people thought of her going there. As athletic as she was, she had spent most of her free time since she was twelve working at the town library as her parents had asked her to do, in preparation for college. Her high school had limited athletic opportunities; it had only started to provide athletic programs for girls after the passage of Title IX in 1972, which banned sex discrimination in educational programs or activities. To prepare she ran and ran. "Back then there weren't strength and conditioning coaches or personal trainers I could go to, so I'd run around the track," she said. "I remember being all bundled up in sweats, cruising around the track and feeling sick to my stomach. I was pushing myself fairly hard. I'm glad I did it, that's how I got ready."

Reporting-in day was somewhat of a blur. She remembers her parents driving her through the gates of the academy in New London, Connecticut, in early July. She wore a nice white dress and carried her bright red suitcase. She was in great shape physically. As she walked toward the archway of Chase Hall (the cadet barracks) to begin her four-year journey, it took her fifty-six steps before the first catcall singed her eardrums. The sound stopped her in her tracks. "I did not expect that. That's not why I came. A sickening chill went through my body as I looked up to see who it was," she said. "Even to this day I remember the window. That was the first indication that something else was going to unfold."

Bibeau said that what waited as she entered the academy was a community, with minor but important exceptions, that did not want women present. Bibeau's swab (freshman) experience was typical of any cadet's grueling summer. Within the first two weeks she knew the lineup. Some upperclassmen were friendly, fair, regular guys. There were even those classmates who were supportive. She had identified them. The rest made it clear that they did not want women at the academy.

The transition was going to be warlike and a day-to-day fight for survival. The gathering of the swabs in Dimick Hall for a summer evening lecture proved to be a warning shot. The cadets were happy about going to the hall because there was air-conditioning and comfortable chairs. Selected first and second class cadets were also present to supervise the swabs. "We were going to listen to a senior, well-respected person and officer discuss life in the Coast Guard. He opened his presentation with a joke," she said. "The joke was, 'Letting women into the academy was like letting your mother-in-law drive your brand new Cadillac off a cliff.' It was like a knife just went through my shoulder blades. It hurt." That safety and security net she thought she had begun to develop was gone. She watched as every male in that lecture hall leaped to his feet in a standing ovation. The girls just sat in their seats. Their jaws dropped, and their bodies sank into their chairs.

"That's when the ground shifted. We started to realize that if you're going to stay here you're going to have to get involved in a different kind of experience. One where you're either going to prove that women can do this and take on that burden for the entire gender or just leave because maybe it's not worth it." Some women did choose to leave rather than fight.

Bibeau deliberated over the next couple of weeks. Her world and her slice of the fight were very small, but they loomed largely in front of her. "It consisted of who I interacted with at any given moment, mostly cadets." She became withdrawn, distrustful. But in the end Bibeau decided that she would take on the challenge and stay. "At least for the time being, for any given twenty-four-hour period I would stay," she said. "There were many, countless times I thought about leaving. Usually it had to do with acceptance." The daily difficulties were fought and overcome with few but welcomed rewards. "We surprised the folks who were nonbelievers," she said. "It was rewarding to see that take place. It was unfortunate that it had to come to that, but rewarding even so."

One of the win-like events took place that summer aboard a training tall ship, USCGC *Eagle*. Bibeau was on a one-week cruise off the New England coast with her classmates, six of whom were women. The ship's company, active duty crewmen who served in the Coast Guard, instructed the cadets on sailing and navigating. They taught them the art of manning sail stations to adjust the massive square sails, some of which were as wide as five king bed sheets, for course changes.

One sunny day, the waters were calm and the captain and ship's company had assembled for a challenge that had been "thrown down." The swabs were told climb up a line left dangling from the first yardarm of the main mast where it had been tied off. It was pretty high and the thick, heavy, rough hemp line made for a tough climb. A few of the swabs felt they were skilled enough to take on the challenge, though not many did. It became clear that the test was also to see if any of the women would go up. "You could feel the pulsing in the crowd. There were no words. There were no taunts. There was this energy," said Bibeau. "I decided I wasn't going to let it go unchallenged."

She studied which of her classmates were going to go up next and that's when she saw Jim Preisig. He didn't appear to be the most athletic of the bunch, and she figured she was not that lacking and got in line behind him. "Jim goes up, but Jim has trouble coming down. He loses his grip and slides down the line taking the skin off his hands as he goes." Next in line, Bibeau stepped up. "My heart was pounding out of my chest as I climbed. I was just not going to let my body give out. It was not going to happen." She made it up and more importantly made it down, learning from Jim's painful example of how not to do it. "There was a cheer that was vastly disproportionate but uplifting compared to the cheer that had gone up for the guys. People were worried. I think there was some fairly enlightened leadership on the ship. There was a kind of breath of relief that they maybe wouldn't have to deal with the talk that woman were less capable than the men and that maybe they'd be just fine." It was a bright, beautiful day and Bibeau's mood matched it. "There was a shift in energy that began to occur at least in that little place at that moment. I learned from it how important physical performance was for my survival. It was one of the tools I could use to escape very harassing behavior over time."

Another diversion that provided her some relief was getting involved with seasonal sports at the academy. Over the next couple of years she helped start the women's gymnastics team and the basketball team, and was involved in sailing in the spring and fall each year. "I was very fortunate to have a coach, [Capt.] Lawson Brigham (Class of 1970 alumni), who didn't care whether you were a boy, girl, purple, or green. He was all about 'Let's go out and sail, win, do a good job.' There was a level of acceptance on the waterfront that didn't exist anywhere else on campus." This spirit of mutual respect among all the sailors enabled Bibeau to become a skipper her junior year and go on to lead the women into the national championships her senior year.

There were many times she could have left but didn't because she was pleased with what she was doing and learning in class. Her sailing team was winning. The promise of a maritime career that was meaningful and one where she would be leading others and not be sitting behind a desk was exactly what she wanted to do.

III

When Paula Thornhill left Sylvania, Ohio, a suburb of Toledo, for the U.S. Air Force Academy in Colorado Springs, Colorado, there was little attention paid by those living there to the news that she would be going to the academy with the first class to include women. There was not a lot of military presence in the region to make the news a big deal either.

Thornhill said her parents had raised their children to identify their goals and pursue them. "The whole idea that you couldn't do something because of ethnicity, gender, or race was just not in our upbringing," said Thornhill. Her father was a World War II veteran who was promoted to corporal twice, having once been knocked down in rank for disobeying orders. Her uncles were also in the service during the war. One of her uncles and his wife were prisoners of war on Borneo for three years, interned by the Japanese. "In many ways I was a product of the Second World War . . . more of a citizen-soldier model than a professional military model," she added as her reason for joining the air force. Going to the academy was not based on a sophisticated calculus for a seventeen-year-old, she said. "This opened up for the first time. Why not try? My concept of military service was not profound. You did it, then got on with life. I decided if it was easier to leave once accepted than get in."

In preparation for the summer initiation boot camp, she worked out frequently. There were very few high school sports available for women, so she ran, lifted weights, and went swimming. "The toughest part is that you just don't know until you get there whether or not you're mentally prepared. How strong is your psyche when you have five people standing at arm's length away yelling at you?" she said. "Until you go through that you just don't know." What she did know was that her family had confidence in her and believed in her goal. Their support would sustain her through the intangibles.

The Class of 1980 started with about 1,500 members, and 10 percent of those were women. Her first days at the Air Force Academy were "equally unsettling" for all the cadets. "I don't think the guys had a good time either. When I think back, the guys really put up with an awful lot because we (the women) were there. Plus they didn't get any of the psychic benefit of people paying attention to them and saying (sarcastically), 'Wow, isn't this amazing that you are doing this?' They are getting dumped on as much or more than we are. They were like, 'Hey, I'm not weaker just because they are here.'"

The number of people who oversaw their leadership and development were split between tormentors, supporters, and nonvoters. "Most everybody was in the middle with a stance of wait and see," Thornhill recalled. "Others would act like we were not there, and some didn't want to be bothered. Those who thought we were okay were not going to come out and say so because they felt their classmates and other officers would think they were weak, lazy, or lame."

Thornhill praised the women in her class, saying they were "unbelievably smart." Some of the women had prior college education, others had prior military service, and some were pretty good athletes. This was noteworthy at a time when women were only beginning to be included in nontraditional careers and athletic programs.

There were numerous times she felt that the women were unnecessarily harassed in a variety of ways. Verbal shouts, or "barking," when guys yelled, "You dumb, ugly bitch," happened on occasion to Thornhill. Another time some upperclassmen went down to the butcher shop and got a cow's head and threw it into the women's shower. "There are all sorts of stories. You look back and say that should not have happened. That was pretty bad. It would be unfair to the institution to say these events dominated my perspective," explained Thornhill. "Certainly when things like that happened you said, 'What's up? This is just weird. This is odd. This is cruel.'" She stands by her belief that the institution and her classmates were better than that. "There were always moments when people slipped. The overall experience was positive, just grueling . . . and I was just focused on surviving."

III

Back east in Annapolis, Disher was also focused on surviving. She had braved the summer's challenges in part by showing that she was an exceptional athlete and fitting in with the guys. She could swear and cut down her female classmates as easily as they could.

Acceptance Day was in her rearview mirror, and during the academic year, she had opportunities to meet some of the other women who were among the thirty-six companies of the Brigade of Midshipmen. Disher learned that these women had equally severe experiences, which varied in intensity, due to the "personalities" of their company. One of her really good friends (identified in her book, *First Class*, as Meredith Britain), a beautiful California girl with a fun personality, was an example. "Her company nearly destroyed her," Disher recalls. She found out that Britain was restricted to her room since the beginning of the semester of their senior year. It was a raw deal. Charged with unauthorized absence, for which midshipmen normally received seventy-five demerits and two month's restriction, Britain had been awarded 150 demerits and six month's restriction. This included reporting to the main office in uniform every two hours. "It was thirty years later at our reunion that she was able to finally say she had overcome the pain of her experience."

The way the teenaged men treated the women was erratic. Some were really hateful in action and in word, vocalizing how they felt with regular insulting confrontations. Some could not care less, having accepted that the law allowed women. Others were interested in dating the women. There was another type that wanted to be friends and help. "They were heroes and very brave to be our friends. It took great courage because they took a lot of garbage on the side to support us and even come to our defense," Disher said. "Two classmates in particular were very supportive and became my good friends. One was a gay guy as it turned out many years later and the other was a black football player." They obviously understood what it was to be a minority at the Naval Academy. In fact, there were more women in the Class of 1980 than there were African Americans.

Disher enjoyed going to football games and had cheered in high school. She was encouraged to continue her passion for cheerleading at the Naval Academy. Before the women were admitted, the academy had women from other colleges cheer their teams on. Disher and six other women tried out and all made it. "Here we are with really short hair, no make up, no jewelry. We look like we're ten years old," she said as they walked out before the brigade (the entire student body) for a game. The naval midshipmen responded with shock. "They were screaming, 'Get off the field. Get out of our school. You guys are ugly. You're fat.' It was horrible at every game. The squad had a cheer, 'A-B-U-S-E, abuse, abuse,' and the midshipmen would shout back, 'O-B-E-S-E, obese, obese,'" said Disher. "We had another cheer, 'Block that kick. Block that kick.' And the guys would yell back at us, 'Suck my dick.' No one did anything about it."

The women cheered the football season of their plebe year and enjoyed getting to go to the away games and getting out of the academy. With a new coach they thought the sophomore season would be better, different. To their dismay it was the same. Cans of soda were thrown at the cheerleaders. They decided to stick it out for the famed Army–Navy Game. Before that day arrived they had practiced a dance routine for the academy pep rally. They ran out to perform it in front of four thousand midshipmen, and the entire place erupted in boos. "'Boo! Boo! Get off our stage! Get out of our school! Boo!'" Disher recalled. "I'm mouthing obscenities as I'm doing this routine. By then I had a real sailor mouth." Backstage they talked about quitting but wanted to support the team. Disher decided that she would cheer the Army–Navy Game so that her friends and family could see her on television and then she would quit.

Meanwhile, the football coach and the superintendent of the academy got up on stage and proceeded with the rest of the rally like nothing had happened. "No one said that's not how you treat a shipmate." On the way back to their rooms someone accosted the cheerleaders with shaving cream, spraying it all over them. "Kids are just stupid when they are that age. Their prefrontal cortex is not formed yet. Their reasoning abilities are gone. It was just mean what they did."

One sparkle of light came for Disher when Phil McConkey, Class of 1978 and the football team captain, who later played for the New York Giants, came up to Disher at a party shortly after the Army–Navy game and said, "Sharon, I just wanted, on behalf of the football players, to thank you guys. I know you put up with a lot of stuff to be out there on the field. I want you to know we really appreciate you all being there. We really wish you wouldn't quit but we understand what you are going through." That meant the *world* to Disher. It was the experience that kept her at the academy, but it was moments like this one when she felt she had made a difference. She loved it. She loved the challenge. She appreciated the camaraderie, her classmates, her systems engineering instructors, and she wanted to serve her country. "I wanted to get the best education I could, and for me, the good moments far outweighed the bad."

Disher said that each midshipman, male or female, had to find a survival mechanism to complete the four-year ordeal. "Of the girls, some became promiscuous. Some turned to religion and some just became wallflowers to hide and blend in. Others had eating disorders. Whatever it took, you had to find a survival mechanism. For me, I would have to say it was trying to become one of the guys and probably also, a first class (senior) guy I dated. Everyone is telling you, 'You're fat. You're ugly. You shouldn't be here.' But then there is this guy, the captain of the lacrosse team and he was hot. And he wanted to date me? That was a real ego booster and really helped me survive the whole ordeal."

III

Nestled along the Hudson River fifty miles north of New York City, Marene Allison had also survived West Point's cadet basic training. The rite of passage of Beast Barracks—the first year Cadet Basic Training—was a memory as she focused ahead on the demanding academic years.

Participating in team sports and leadership training were two important elements in addition to her core concentration in engineering studies. Women's team sports did not exist yet at the academy. Her roommate encouraged her to take up orienteering, an international running sport of navigation from point to point through a forest using a map and compass. "It's like a marathon in the woods," said Allison. "You have to make decisions on the fly. It's a thinking sport." This gave her a little escape from the drills and ceremonies. The experience also provided more time off West Point on weekends to enjoy the outdoors and refocus her strength and perseverance.

She carefully evaluated the interactions she had with her colleagues. Twelve of the thirty-six companies now included eight to ten women. Knowing who was going to be in their company for the next few years enabled the plebes to bond a little more. "I call that phase of being a cadet more like the CBS television show *Survivor*. Who's the leader? Who's in charge? Who's going to build the hut? Who's going to create fire? The storming and norming that goes on in that show reminds me what it was like as a plebe. Everybody's feeling his or her way out, who's going to survive and who's going to be voted off the island."

She noticed that as second-year students, they no longer had the sense of protection that they had experienced as the most junior class. "You thought people just didn't talk to you because you were a plebe and that's fine. As you moved up they would just openly say things to you: 'You shouldn't be here.

You've ruined the Corps. You're awful. You're a tramp.' They'd say this stuff to your face. You always felt like a red-headed stepchild."

Some of her classmates were supportive of the women while others chose to ignore them. The guys who "got" being a cadet treated the women well. It seemed to Allison that those who struggled to exist came to hate the women. "If you read about minority groups they say this happens with minorities comparing themselves to other minorities."

There were a number of times that her female peers were sexually harassed or assaulted, says Allison. During her yearling (sophomore) year she was alone in her room studying on a Saturday night. A guy who she thought was dating her roommate came in her room and started "semi-attacking" me. "He grabbed me. I just gave him a good knee to the groin and yelled, 'Get the hell out of my room.' The thing was there was no way to report it. Nobody had talked to cadets about how to report sexual assault. It was like they assumed none of it would ever occur because they're cadets. Everything would be fine." Another woman was raped. The woman reported it and left the academy. "The guy was never brought up on charges and ended up graduating. I had a good friend of mine, who worked in a position of trust at the academy. Through her position she was aware of a number of women who had either been assaulted or raped, but most were not acted upon because many of [the cases] had an element of drinking, which makes things messier."

Allison discovered that not taking the long-term view, just taking one day at a time and making it through to the next was a healthy approach.

III

Further north in New London, Bibeau had also completed her swab summer and was well into the freshman academic year. With so few women at the Coast Guard Academy, the superintendent decided that women would live in half of the Corps' companies. That way they each would have a roommate. "From my perspective, there was a very unfortunate dynamic between the half of the Corps that had women and the half that did not," said Bibeau. "The half that did was learning to appreciate each other. They were getting through the conversation that women don't belong here and saying, 'Well, maybe things are just fine.'" The other half, those without women in their ranks, led by the Class of 1979, was on a different trajectory. "They were all about restoring things to the way they used to be. The dynamic became very unhealthy."

One morning in December 1978 the ill feelings were made perfectly clear with a regimental instruction. The cadets awoke to find a memo taped to their doors designed to "dispel all rumors that the United States Coast Guard Academy has become pussy whipped over the past 2.5 years." Under the action paragraph of the memo was the direction that "cadets shall return to the overall and basic functions, activities and attitudes reminiscent of the period 1964–1974 at the Academy" and that "the following specific items will no longer be deemed as in bad taste" including, "gross out nights, crude and abusive language, clothes optional while enroute to and from heads, all heads are to become co-ed as of 1 Jan. 1979 based on the premise that separate cannot be equal." Finally, "resignation papers may be picked up in the yeoman's office."

"There was this enormous fishbowl affect," said Bibeau. "Every move that every woman made was seen as typecast for her gender. That's what women do, that's what they don't do. The upper class seemed to have something to prove."

Bibeau had something to prove too. "I could outrun most of the guys, and they didn't mess with me for the most part." She realized there were ways in addition to being physically strong that she could cope. She made it through the next couple of years with the strength of truth. "I survived by staying true to what is true," she said. "This was harassing behavior. That was true. I believed things would ease up the last year there. All in all I discovered I could often insulate myself from it by being physically competent and standing by the truth."

The third mechanism she used to survive was to put what happened in the rearview mirror. She focused on what needed to be done that day and the next without hanging on to the stress of what she had moved past.

III

Between her sophomore and junior year, Thornhill had seriously considered leaving the Air Force Academy but not because of the hostile climate. "The principal reason was that I wasn't sure I could do enough in the air force as a career. I went to the academy with bad eyesight and knew I could not fly. This normally would not be a big deal, but in this culture, flying is everything. At this point, I'm nineteen. I'm not stupid. Do I want to enter a career where it's pretty obvious I'm going to be a second-class citizen from the time of my commission?" She wrestled with that issue. Working through it with the support of her family, she decided to stay.

One of the lessons she learned from the academy experience was how to manage life's demands and "fail gracefully." She explained, "Life is a marathon. You've got to pace yourself. You quickly figure out that there are always people more talented than you in some areas, so the competition becomes with yourself not with somebody else." She was thankful that "the academy opened up doors I didn't even understand existed."

III

Hanley, Allison, Bibeau, and Thornhill agree their final year was far easier than the previous three. Despite the vocal minority who didn't want them to graduate, they were able to adjust and survive. The women triumphed academically and militarily, and soon would realize their goal of becoming commissioned officers in May 1980.

There were similarities in their experiences. Decades later the women were able to meet on a few occasions with their fellow female cadets and discuss issues, such as uniforms not fitting correctly or other mundane topics, and make progress. The clothing issues were resolved. Yet, with the real tough issues of assault or harassment, "that was dangerous territory," recalled Bibeau of her experience in the Coast Guard Academy. "The consequence was that often we didn't know what was happening to one another. It was very difficult. We were just kids, ages seventeen, eighteen, nineteen. None of us were equipped to talk about or deal with these issues, and the academy was not equipped to deal with them either."

Disher says at Annapolis, "I made it a point to never get together with the girls because I didn't want it to be seen like a sewing circle where the girls get together. This was really too bad because we could have been a great source of comfort and support for each other, but we didn't do that." She said one of the girls did try to gather all the women together one evening and got caught. She was called to see the commandant of cadets and he almost threw her out. It was grounds for mutiny.

Allison said her most difficult challenge at West Point was not academic or military requirements. She felt it was dealing with the fact that men didn't really want women there. For Bibeau, the most difficult challenge was the "unrelenting nature of the surprises. You never knew when someone was going to do something stupid or when the next memo was going to be placed on the door."

"The process of change was unfolding—ugly moments and all. The reason I bring it up now is for two reasons," Bibeau explained. "One, that history has been forgotten and two, there's a risk of repeating it with the repeal of the Don't Ask Don't Tell policy. Unless we learn from the lessons of the past, the past is destined to be repeated. No one would be proud of it." As she matured and progressed though her successful career, Bibeau realized that sometimes you have to put a name on these behaviors in order for things to really change. "It's not enough to do your best. It's not enough to set a good example. The organization also has to grow up," she added, knowing that there will be a whole new meaning to this as gays openly serve in the military.

Academy women were thrust into the media spotlight from Acceptance Day to graduation. The press created a problem by focusing attention on the women, diminishing their coverage of the men's achievements. Ironically, this fishbowl effect of increased attention and reporting on the women fueled and encouraged the male animosity.

Shortly after Bibeau began her senior year at the Coast Guard Academy, reporters arrived to interview the women about what they planned to do after graduation. She said it was a habit by now for the academy to call the women to a conference room for the press interview. There were no public affairs officers to guide the questions and support the women. "We were all guarded about what we said publicly even though we had a number of experiences the public would probably not find acceptable."

The *Day* reporter from New London was apparently pretty savvy. Instead of writing about what their careers would be after graduation, to their dismay he wrote about the women's experiences at the Coast Guard Academy in a way that was misleading and claimed harassment in such a way that the story nearly led to their dismissal.

Bibeau said of course there's an enormous amount of harassment that occurred, but they didn't talk about it much back then especially to the public. When the article ran, "we felt set up and used. Talk about that sinking feeling in your stomach." The women were informed of the story at ten o'clock that night and were called into the commandant of cadets' office, a terrifying experience. The senior officer grilled them asking, "How could we possibly do this? There's no sexual harassment at the academy." "We're looking at him like, 'What planet do you live on?'" Bibeau could not understand why, after they were thrown into a room with reporters and the commandant of cadets had not provided them a facilitator or public affairs representative, he then accused them of saying something they had not said and held them accountable. "There were so many dark, difficult days getting through that. We had a good six months to go. It was time to climb out of the nose dive."

The November 1979 issue of the *Washingtonian* ran an article by James Webb, an ex-marine and Naval Academy graduate, titled "Women Can't Fight." Disher recalled during this interview and in her book that the article evoked a variety of "piercing comments from the men" who continued to believe that women did not belong at the academy and "thank God somebody finally had the balls to say so." Webb went so far as to write that placing women at the service academies was "poisoning the preparation of men for combat command by sexually sterilizing the Naval Academy environment in the name of equality." He continued, although only "three major conduct offenses for sexual fraternization" had been documented in the three years women had been there, it was Webb's opinion that "sex was commonplace in Bancroft Hall." He also interviewed and quoted three male midshipmen from the Class of 1980 and one from the Class of 1979 who opined that women were given preferential treatment and that this was a concern for the welfare of the military and the country.

Webb could not have been more wrong, said Disher, who believed another reason for the women's cold reception was partially based on policy. The combat exclusion policy prohibited women in the Department of Defense from being assigned to combat units. This conflicted with the academy's mission. "We weren't allowed to go into combat situations, and yet we were training to be combat leaders," said Disher. "We were constantly bombarded with, 'You're taking the place of some guy who could really serve this country. You shouldn't be here because you can't serve in the capacity that you're being trained to.'" She said that in response she'd reply, "'Yes, it was true, but now that there are women trained to be combat leaders, let's start looking at opening up some fields for them.' We paved the way in respect to that and it took a long time."

In fact, navy women were first assigned to select noncombatant ships in 1978, midway through their academy journey. The Coast Guard, part of the Department of Transportation at the time, also lifted all restrictions for women aboard their ships around the same time.

The secretary of the air force, in 1985, announced changes to the combat exclusion policy to allow women to serve as forward air controllers, fly and crew various models of the C-130 aircraft, and to serve at munitions storage facilities. It was nearly two decades later, in 1994, that navy women were assigned to billets in surface combatants. The Department of Defense's policy continues to prevent women from being assigned to ground combat units below the brigade level. The navy is planning for the first group of female submarine officers and female warfare-qualified supply officers to be assigned to four submarines in December 2011. The twenty-four female officers, many of them graduates from Annapolis with engineering degrees, attended the navy's submarine and nuclear power schools.

III

On May 28, 1980, ninety-seven graduates were the first women to receive commissions as second lieutenant during graduation ceremonies at the Air Force Academy. Paula Thornhill was among them and proudly went on to serve in the air force until 2009. Among many notable assignments, she was the special assistant to the chairman of the Joint Chiefs of Staff at the Pentagon, assigned to the Office of the Secretary of Defense, and earned a master's degree in history from Stanford University and a doctorate in history from Oxford University. She was promoted to the rank of brigadier general before retiring to work for Rand Corporation, a nonpartisan, nonprofit global research and analysis institution.

Thornhill returned to the Air Force Academy in 1985 as a history instructor and executive officer to the dean of the faculty. She said this job was more unpleasant than being a cadet. "Some of the most unprogressive attitudes toward women were resident in some of the departments on the faculty. Why? Who knows," she added. "My guess is that they didn't change over that much. When you have a mission to accomplish you don't have a lot of time to think about who's doing it." She explained that the institution needed to go through two big changes, which could not be accomplished in a mere four years. The obvious one was changing over the cadet wings so that women were assigned to each of wings, or living areas. The second was an organizational change of the staff and faculty, a much slower process.

Marene (Nyberg) Allison walked as a member of the long gray line across the graduation stage at West Point. Sixty-two of the 119 women who reported in 1976 graduated and were commissioned.

After completing her five-year commitment, Allison decided to leave the army at the rank of captain. She had married an army officer and together they had a son. The couple decided to become special agents in the Federal Bureau of Investigation. She worked on drug operations and had a number of large cases in which "bad people were put in jail for distributing large quantities of cocaine in the United States." In the mid-nineties she began her corporate work in information technology security. Avaya, a global leader in business communications, hired her in 2002. She was responsible for intrusion detection of the World Cup Network that same year. Recruited to be chief security officer at Medco, a health care company, she worked there until August 2010 when she moved over to Johnson and Johnson as vice president of worldwide information security.

Allison is the president of West Point Women, a network of academy women who support each other as cadets and graduates. Quarterly newsletters, articles, and meetings provide opportunities for women from as far away as Hawaii to Washington, D.C., to come together and mentor each other. One of the reasons she's been active with West Point Women is of the lack of fellowship she experienced with other women as a cadet and officer. "Sometimes you need to talk to someone with perspective, and we help to connect those who can help with those seeking it."

On March 2, 2011, the U.S. Army Women's Foundation announced its Hall of Fame inductees for 2011: the first women graduates of the United States Military Academy at West Point, Class of 1980.

Susan (Donner) Bibeau was one of fourteen females to graduate with the Coast Guard Academy's Class of 1980. She served six years at sea and was the commanding officer of two patrol boats, the *Cape Henlopen* and the *Maui*. She was executive assistant to the Pacific area commander, among other notable assignments during her thirty-year career before returning to the Coast Gaurd Academy as director of admissions. She married and had two children. Capt. Bibeau retired in March 2010 after nine successful years. She plans to begin her civilian career in student development at another Connecticut college, helping to improve graduation rates for underserved students.

Coming back to the academy as director of admissions, Bibeau noticed that the tension between men and women cadets she had felt as a student was not present and the number of women had grown. She knew that, along with her classmates, "we had set the stage for this evolution to occur . . . [and] that was very rewarding."

But she also observed that many of her classmates from the 1980s were now making up the senior cadre and permanent teaching staff at the academy. "A lot of the same baggage was present with this group. In many ways our thinking has not matured." The patterns between interactions of men and women were still unhealthy on the staff and officer level she says. "Now, I think the challenge for the Coast Guard is to recognize those patterns and eradicate them. The idea of inclusionary leadership is still maturing. Control and authority can be shared without the threat between people who are very different from each other. Justice Sandra Day O'Connor has said in affirmative action cases that 'thirty years goes by in a heart beat.' It's really not that long when you're talking about organizational change. We got so busy congratulating ourselves on the fact that we opened doors to women that we forgot to do all the hard work that's involved in the maturation process. Let the light shine on the history. Let's understand it."

Bibeau says service academies are "amazing opportunities for people. The question is, is it right for you?" She believes the question that women want to consider, because they are still the minority at all the service academies and services, is not only how will it feel but also what will you be doing when you graduate. She says it is very important to be aware of whom you will be working with after graduation, more so than where in the country you will be living.

"My decision to go to the academy definitely shaped the rest of my life. I'm very glad that I went. I've gained a lot in many, many ways because of it . . . ways not always expected."

Sharon (Hanley) Disher was the first woman to graduate from the Naval Academy with a degree in systems engineering. Found medically disqualified from flying because of a depth perception deficiency, with her engineering major she was a natural for the Civil Engineering Corps. Assigned tours of duty in South Carolina, New Orleans, and Everett, Washington, she was also the officer in charge of Construction Battalion Unit 414 in New London, Connecticut. After living in Madrid, Spain, for four years, the Disher family returned to live in Annapolis, where she currently runs an afterschool engineering and science program for underserved children.

Disher said the academy and navy experiences were definitely worth the challenge. "It's a great leadership opportunity and a way to give back by serving your country," she said. "I think everybody should be required to serve their country in some capacity." Sharon Hanley Disher, her twin children Alison and Brett, and their dad, Tim Disher, are all Naval Academy graduates. Youngest son Matthew is a member of the Naval Academy Class of 2013. The Disher family is the first in American history to send every member to Annapolis.

12

Bringing Light to the Darkness of the Deep

Capt. Gina Harden, USN

It's not good if you are not scared.
You'd better be because you're on your toes if you are.

Fortitude. Intestinal fortitude. That's how Capt. Gina Harden, who became a U.S. Navy diver in 1982, came to describe her ability to endure and serve in the elite corps of divers within the military special operations community. When Harden trained for qualification, the dive program used rigs such as the Mark V, with diving helmet, boots, and gear that weighed almost two hundred pounds dry. Another fifty or more pounds were added when the rig filled up with water to about the diver's neck. Fortunately, the internal air pressure in the helmet kept the water below Harden's mouth, enabling her to clear her ears during descent and still communicate with the controllers on the surface. This type of rig was a memorable prop in the 2000 film *Men of Honor*, in which Cuba Gooding Jr. portrayed the navy's first African-American master diver, Master Chief Carl Brashear. Brashear was also the first amputee navy diver to be recertified, after proving he could walk the required number of steps wearing the oppressive load.

Harden did not quit when the physical and mental demands nearly overwhelmed her during dive school. Instead she pressed forward with self-confidence and willpower to qualify as the navy's seventh woman diver. Navy divers are accustomed to going deep, working hard in zero visibility with chain saws and hydraulic tools while battling dangerous conditions to complete harrowing missions. Harden was attracted to this world of work and was enthralled by the opportunities afforded to a navy diver, including deep-sea underwater salvage of aircraft and ships, harbor-clearance operations, in-water ship demolition operations, underwater construction, and welding. She learned that navy divers also conduct submarine repairs and rescue and were skilled adventurers serving as diving technical experts for SEAL, Marine Corps, and navy Explosive Ordnance Disposal (EOD) diving commands around the globe.

For three decades Harden has been one of the few women leaders in this community and participated in some of the most historic, groundbreaking dives on military record. One such mission was an archeological effort with the National Oceanic and Atmospheric Administration (NOAA) to salvage portions of the Civil War ironclad USS *Monitor*. "The highlight of my career was the two summers diving on the USS *Monitor* in 2001 and 2002," said Harden. "It was incredibly challenging and exhilarating." The *Monitor*, an armored gunboat with a revolving turret, battled the ironclad CSS *Virginia* on March 9, 1862 in the Battle of Hampton Roads, which heralded the beginning of a new era in naval warfare, marking the change from wood and sail to iron and steam ships. While being towed off North Carolina's Outer Banks, in the Graveyard of the Atlantic, the ship sank during a storm on December 31, 1862. For 111 years its resting place was a mystery, until it was discovered in 1973. The wreck site was designated the Monitor National Marine Sanctuary—the first such sanctuary in the United States—and managed by NOAA, who partnered with the U.S. Navy for its underwater salvage and recovery expertise to survey the wreck site and recover a number of artifacts.

Recovering elements of the ship—including the first 360-degree revolving gun turret, two Dahlgren cannons, engine, condenser, shaft, and screw—was dangerous and deep. Located sixteen miles south-southeast of Cape Hatteras, the area rips with powerful ocean currents. At 240 feet underwater, the mission called for some of the deepest work in the roughest seas. Because of the distance from the dive platform, Harden, a surface-supply diver who returned to the surface after each dive, would have to breathe a special prescription mix of helium and oxygen while working below. After returning to the dive barge she would step into the surface decompression chamber to return her body to normal pressures—a process that could take as long as three hours and fifteen minutes. In contrast, the saturation divers who helped with the re-covery remained at the deep dive pressure and lived and worked for nine days in a pressurized world, and then spent three days decompressing. By using a saturation bell—a living area that was lowered during the day to the sea floor and carried up to the dive barge at night—they could remain at their desired depth and pressure for nearly two weeks without having to decompress to a surface air pressure.

Harden and her fellow divers brought imposing tools down to the deep with them for the precision work needed to remove the gun turret. Their job required delicacy, to avoid destroying the precious artifact, and toughness, to cut through the reinforced iron hull. The hydroblaster, with its 20,000-pound-per-square-inch water jet, cut through metal along with a hydraulic chisel. An exothermic torch—which sends out an arc of fire requiring 440 volts of electricity made by burning a mixture of oxygen and magnesium—also came in handy to blast away at the ship's hull and armor belt that landed on top of the turret when the *Monitor* flipped over and landed upside down in its final resting place 140 years before. Harden and her dive partner were assigned the task of placing wood two-by-fours between the ironclad's revolving gun turret and the "spider," or expanding claw-like metal hook used to pull the turret off the bottom.

The divers were only allowed to stay on the bottom for a short time. After descending from the surface on a stage or platform, clearing their ears all the way to avoid rupturing an eardrum, they hovered thirty feet above the *Monitor*. "You have to throw your umbilical [air hose] over the side of the stage and essentially run through the water to the *Monitor*," said Harden. "For twenty minutes on the bottom, it's quite an ordeal." She had ten blocks of two-by-fours tied together with polypropylene rope trailing behind her in the water. "I'm trying to tow them to the turret, and I looked like Medusa! The turret is about nine feet tall. I'm five feet four, and I'm standing in this trench looking up about thirteen feet, wondering, *How am I going to get to the top?*" Harden started jumping. She tried to climb up the spider and could not get a grip. "I said [in a high-pitched, helium-induced voice] to Topside [the dive supervi-sors on the barge], 'I can't get on top of the turret.'" Eventually, Topside instructed her to go over to the other diver who was on top of the turret and climb up his umbilical, and she succeeded.

"Going to that depth, out in the middle of the ocean, it's kind of surreal," Harden explained. Besides the problem of her ears adjusting to the depth, there's inherent performance pressure to descend to the bottom as quickly as possible. She had to clear her ears all the way down and answer occasional requests from Topside: "Red Diver [as one of the two divers is traditionally called], can we speed it up?" If she or another diver experienced an "ear squeeze" on the way down, or were unable to clear the pressure building up in the eardrum, they would have to abort the dive. Setting up for a replacement diver can take hours.

If something happened while down in the deep, Harden's escape plan would have included trying to make it to the saturation bell. "You're only down there with one come-home bottle of air, which is not enough to make it to the surface," she explained. "The saturation bell stayed on the bottom and was at dive pressure during surface-supplied diving operations. There was always a danger that something could go wrong." Besides losing your air supply, other dangers included having a physical problem with the depth, getting the bends (decompression sickness), or being pulled away by the rough seas or swift two to nine knot currents that sometimes raced through the site. There were many other dangers that put the divers at risk: suffering hypothermia due to the cold water temperatures, having the air supply hose caught or cut on metal debris, having something fall on top of the diver or air hose and crushing it, falling into the turret, and even undergoing complications while recovering the dive stage, or the platform that took them to the surface. "It's not good if you are not scared," she said. "You'd better be scared because you're on your toes if you are."

One of the joys of being part of a historic recovery of a naval artifact was the sense of patriotism and respect Harden felt for the sixteen of the sixty-two American crewmen who did not survive the *Monitor*'s sinking. "We found the remains of two of them, which were sent to forensic specialists. You can't help but think about the sailors on that navy ship. There's a feeling of kinship for them." Harden and the team of divers took down "challenge coins" (coins given to military members in appreciation for their exemplary service) they had designed for the mission to hide in the wreck. On one side was an image of Poseidon, Greek god of the sea, and on the other an image of a navy diver, both pulling on the turret. Their patriotism was displayed in full measure. "We had a flag flying on the *Monitor*—everybody took their flag down to fly."

Women have succeeded in many navy fields not normally open to women, but women navy diving officers are still rare. In fact, among enlisted sailors only one female has achieved the qualification of master diver. Officers who graduate from the Navy Diving and Salvage Training Center are called diving officers, and because Harden also qualified as a salvage officer she is a diving and salvage officer. Harden has also achieved something intangible. She was able to keep her feminine style in a man's world and prove an equal match without having to change and act like a man. "I'm not a threatening person. I usually don't say a lot. I just do. I think there are a lot of women who think they have to act like a man. I don't think you are successful if you lead like that."

Her style is that of a humble and receptive leader who's not afraid to make decisions. Until the moment when she is required to make a decision, "when the rubber meets the road," she relies on her own sense of empowering those around her to be successful. "Where I work now, I have an operations person and an operations support person. Both can step in and do my job. I always look for counsel and sift through it. I'm not afraid to say I don't have all the answers or all the information." Harden admits that she does hold people accountable and that the backbone of the navy is the senior enlisted personnel she trusts with mentoring the younger sailors.

Harden was inducted into the Women Divers Hall of Fame (WDHOF) in 2003. This hall of fame includes pioneers, leaders, innovators, and world record holders throughout the international diving community. She proudly helps mentor other females coming through the ranks as a member of this organization, which also awards scholarships. The camaraderie that is shared among the women of WDHOF is something they purposely cultivate and find rewarding. "There are several navy divers who have been inducted into the WDHOF, and we are all very close and have a deep appreciation for the character and commitment we all have endured to be successful in a male-dominated career field," said Harden.

Despite all that she has proven she can do, Harden, who still dives and re-certifies every six months, admits, "Every time I get in the water, just because I am a woman, I have to prove myself." She had a young sailor, a "kid," on a dive with her once. He looked over toward her and asked, "Ma'am, are you comfortable with this?" "I just looked at him and said, 'I've used every single dive rig the navy has, Sonny, except one. I think I'm okay." (Harden dived using the Jack Browne, Mark V, 12, 16, 20, and 21 rigs.) Harden believes that the only way to prove yourself is by your performance. She offers this advice: "You are just as good as any other person that's doing the job, be it a man or a woman. People change slowly, and as women we need to have the receptiveness and patience to wait for it [change] to occur and then appreciate it."

Harden was commissioned an ensign in the navy in 1981 after graduating from Florida State University with a degree in movement science and physical education and completing Officer Candidate School. She was a competitive swimmer and college athlete, and very comfortable in the water. She would need to be in order to manipulate the cumbersome diving gear. One of the most difficult tests she would take during her time at the Naval Diving and Salvage Training Center in Panama City, Florida, was a seemingly simple exercise of climbing the pool ladder wearing the rig. The feat was difficult because even when the water slowly drained out of the rig as the diver gradually rose, two hundred pounds of gear was still there to shoulder. Each step up the ladder was laborious and failure could lead to dismissal. "There was a lot of technique to this—learning how to do it," said Harden. "I made up my mind I was going to do it by powering through it." With a lot of people on the deck encouraging her, matched by her willpower, Harden persevered and avoided the humiliation of having a crane come and pluck her up from the ladder.

Harden was the only female in her dive class of thirty-five that began the three-month, grueling curriculum. All through the training and Hell Week—when the students are attacked by the instructors and their masks are pulled off underwater—instructors tried to separate the divers, a violation of a golden rule of diving: never leave your buddy. At that time the school did not have a female locker room, so Harden would hurry to a storage cabinet to change while her dive buddy, who suffered in extra measure because he was partnered with a female, was in the men's locker room. "The instructors would wait to catch us apart," Harden laughed slightly. "We'd then be told to do a hundred four-count flutter kicks on our backs on the pool deck because I was a woman and an additional hundred four-count flutter kicks because my dive buddy couldn't get rid of me. . . . I just would not quit. You roll with it. You did it." Harden held on. She was the top swimmer with a strong upper body and also a good runner. It helped that she could do a lot of pull-ups and push-ups, the signature test of strength and usually a weak area for women.

Even harder to beat was the culture. Harden admitted that there were a lot of men who did not want women to go through dive school and earn a place in the special operations community of highly trained and skilled technicians who deploy all over the world as experts in explosives, diving, and parachuting. "The community is a very testosterone-heavy environment," she explained. "It takes a lot of courage to do it." Nevertheless, she proved herself and earned respect by doing it rather than just talking about it. Her tactic toward those who continued to believe women could not compete or even those who simply did not want women to do the job? "You recognize who they are and carry on."

Carry on, she did. Harden and the eleven remaining classmates graduated from dive school in January 1982. "That was incredibly challenging," she said of her proudest moment as an officer. Next she moved to Newport, Rhode Island, and completed the U.S. Navy's Surface Warfare Officers School to continue her professional education, sharpening her leadership and professional skills in preparation for a sea duty assignment. Sea duty assignments for women had just opened up, and only a few women were assigned to ships. Harden instead chose to attend the police academy for shore patrol operations to develop and conduct an intensive physical fitness curriculum for the U.S. Navy Master-at-Arms' sailors (the navy's police force).

After four years on active duty and a promotion to the rank of lieutenant, Harden left active duty for the navy reserves. Her civilian career expanded overseas with her acceptance into an American exchange program at Robert Gordon University in Aberdeen, Scotland, where she earned a bachelor of science with honors in physical therapy. She practiced physical therapy at the Orlando VA Medical Center in Florida. "Most of the really exciting things I've been able to do I did in the reserves," said Harden. "I can be mobilized and go anywhere."

Of her favorite adventures as a reservist, her assignment as the commanding officer of Mobile Diving and Salvage Unit (MDSU) Two Detachment 608 stands out. Located at the time in Mayport, Florida, Harden led the unit's thirty-five men and women from 2001 to 2002. The navy has two active duty MDSUs, both with a reserve complement. MDSU One is located in Pearl

Harbor, Hawaii, and MDSU Two is in Norfolk, Virginia. Harden has supported both. The mission of the MDSUs was originally to clear harbors and
waterways during the Vietnam War. The units also provide "combat ready and
rapidly deployable diving and salvage teams" for underwater search and rescue and emergency repairs for specialized diving missions in all environments.
Unique operations have included the search and recovery of Trans World Air-
lines Flight 800 near Long Island, New York; the Minneapolis bridge collapse
in 2007; and the sinking of the Japanese fishing vessel *Ehime Maru*.

On February 9, 2001, the submarine USS *Greeneville* and the *Ehime
Maru*, a fishery training ship from Japan, collided off the south coast of Oahu,
Hawaii, while USS *Greeneville* was demonstrating the sub's emergency surfac-
ing ability. The *Ehime Maru* sank within minutes, tragically claiming the lives
of nine people, including four high school students, out of a crew of thirty-
five. Harden was part of the command post assigned to the navy's Pacific Fleet
commander for the recovery of the fishing vessel eight months later. She did
one dive on the ship in order to identify and mark hot tap locations for hazardous material removal and lifting pin (a tool needed to remove the object
or waste from the sea) removal and repair. "The ship was full of fuel, and we
were going to have to tap into compartments from the outside and pump out
hazardous waste." It seemed to Harden that there was some resistance from
the leadership at MDSU One to her and another female diver on the ship. "I
don't know whether it was because we were females or reservists. We eventually got into the water."

For most of the operation she coordinated the missions with eleven supporting operational cells (including MDSU One) and several government
agencies, including Japanese officials and the Japanese Maritime Defense
Force. Harden was disappointed not to get in the water more but found it
very rewarding to be part of the recovery and to work with the Japanese
families. MDSU One recovered the remains of eight of the nine lost as well as
their personal effects. "When I dove I descended past a ring buoy tied to one
of the rails by the ship's fo'c'sle. It was floating upwards with the name *Ehime
Maru* circling it," said Harden of the memory. "One of the divers found the
wedding ring of one of the crewmembers that went down with the ship. He
presented it to the crewmember's wife." The Japanese families, who during

their time of loss and grief took up a collection for the Pentagon Relief Fund right after September 11, humbled Harden.

Harden's favorite expression to explain how she lives her life is from Henry David Thoreau: "I wanted to live deep and suck out all the marrow of life." Adopting this as her motto, Harden likes to maximize every opportunity and lives her life to the fullest. When she reflects upon her life she knows that she has truly lived. Harden admits to having taken full advantage of the opportunities that crossed her path. Capt. Harden continues to serve in the navy as the executive officer and senior military representative for the Department of the U.S. Navy Explosive Safety Inspections Program for Naval Ordnance Safety and Security Activity (NOSSA) in Indian Head, Maryland. In December 2008 Harden was mobilized and served in Afghanistan, traveling all over the combat zone to be an advocate for more than two thousand sailors who were there working for the U.S. Army. Harden was their commander in a combat zone. She ensured the members were trained before they went into theater, assisted with their deployments, made sure they were paid, and helped them move to their needed locations, whether they were detainee guards or yeomen. In recognition of her contributions and for logging over 9,200 miles outside the wire at significant personal risk by ground convoy and fixed-wing and rotary aircraft to "ensure the needs of boots on the ground sailors were met," Harden was awarded the Bronze Star in 2009. She exhibited "Meritorious Service in connection with combat operations against the enemy while serving as Officer In Charge of U.S. Naval Forces Central Command Forward Headquarters, Afghanistan."

Her civilian career has been equally full of adventures. In 2006 she began her work as an employee of BAE Systems, a global defense and security company, and was mission coordinator of force protection and vulnerability assessment teams worldwide. In 2010 she became the program director, supervising more than 120 people and monitoring their research and reports. The teams were constantly traveling and working in hazardous environments or areas of conflict. Her extremely busy schedule meant she made good money but "there's not time to date or even have a puppy," she said. "You give up some things, and you get other things." One of the things she regrets is not having a family of her own. Her three sisters all have children, so she appreciates what they are experiencing and acknowledges that not having children is what she sacrificed to become a naval officer and very successful businesswoman. She was motivated by her parents, her most inspirational role models. Hardworking people, Harden says, they married young. Her mom, a navy wife, kept Harden and her three sisters together and taught them the importance of family. As a result, she is very close to her siblings and parents. She recognized that her mom overcame many challenges while supporting her dad through his navy career. It was not easy to move every two or three years and remain a tight-knit family. Harden's father joined the navy at seventeen years old because his own father had passed suddenly and he needed to work to support his mom and siblings. He enlisted as an airplane mechanic and retired as the force master chief of recruiting, or one level below the master chief of the U.S. Navy. "The good things about me are because of them," says Harden. As for her future, she hopes to swim the English Channel, a childhood dream, and contemplates hiking Peru's Machu Picchu.

Harden has only praise for the navy and wants young women to know that the service has done an outstanding job giving women opportunities to go into any area or specialty, provided they meet the requirements. She advises, "Don't limit yourself or listen to the limitations. You're capable of anything you have the desire to be successful in, so press forward and prepare yourself if there is something you want to achieve." Harden particularly praises the navy for not making special concessions for females and does not believe there should be concessions. "If you are able to qualify then you deserve to be there," she said. "Opening up submarines to women was huge."

Did Harden ever think she would fail to achieve her goals? "Sure, of course," she said. "To me, we are presented with opportunities, and we are led in certain directions as a result. I was in church one time and the sermon was about baby eagles. The mother makes a nest very soft. After the eagles are born she starts to remove the soft stuff and the nest gets uncomfortable for the babies and they eventually fly away. When life gets uncomfortable, I think maybe I'm supposed to go another way. If I fail, I try not to think of it as failure but that this wasn't my intended path."

Afterword

Changing the Rules of Engagement is a collection of timeless leadership stories about courageous, trailblazing military women. Their voices serve as testimony for everyone to strive for changing the rules to cultivate a culture of empowerment in business and in life.

I appreciate you taking the time to read my book or to listen to my audiobook to learn about the positive impacts that result from women and men working together, evolving together—empowering each other.

This endeavor is endless and necessary for businesses to succeed and for people to rise and achieve their goals and dreams in life.

I learned something special from each of the women in my book. Their experiences resonated with me. They helped me grow and rise to face new challenges even though my career in the U.S. Coast Guard was already well underway. I was successful, and yet they taught me to look at my life, my leadership, and my future with a new lens and from a new perspective—something that we all can relate to no matter our phase or place in life.

I'd like to share with you a couple of examples from my book that I found personally life changing for me. I believe they will resonate with you whether you are in business, a student, an entrepreneur, or in the military.

Pam Melroy, astronaut and U.S. Air Force veteran, was driven. Driven as a young girl to become an astronaut when no other woman had done so before. So she took her own path, an original path, and created a path for the next generation to follow. Melroy was only one of three women to fly and command the NASA space shuttles.

Pam's leadership advice rings true across all fields and industries. She knew she needed to understand how different people were going to react to different environments. "It was tough being a woman," she said. "Your credibility was not very high. You had to prove yourself all the time." She was tested again and again and learned a lot about human nature.

"You continually evolve to higher and higher levels. The highest form basically revolves around who you are," said Pam. "You have to get it from within, all the key elements of your personality, as opposed to anything anybody else can impose on you."

She carved her range of leadership and style by reaching outside her comfort zone to shape it. For each and every situation she was in, she was aware of the leadership manner that would work best: dictatorial, demanding, or consensus building, a pep talk or simply letting people do what they do best and staying out of their way. Pam understood who she was as an individual and utilized her knowledge, her leadership range to help others achieve success.

Mattie Wells, a senior enlisted leader and command master chief serving aboard three U.S. Navy warships. I'm particularly fond of Mattie's story. She came from a small town like me and had no money. Her wealth came from within. She had a resolute vision of where she could go and who she could be. She left her small Louisiana town and sailed the seas around the world with the U.S. Navy. Rising to the highest enlisted rank, she worked hard, to the best of her ability to achieve this promotion. Her work ethic resonates with people who work in civilian jobs for a small business or a large corporation.

Another woman whose words resonated with me is Heather A. Wilson, former congressional representative and U.S. Air Force secretary. When Heather said to me, "Dream your bigger dream," I stopped and really took in the significance of those four words.

I know that I grew up with a dream. So have you. In my TEDx and other keynote speeches I've given around the nation at graduations, in leadership symposiums, or for corporate events, I encourage audiences to answer these questions:

What is one thing you've always wanted to do and haven't done yet?

How would your life be different or how can it change today if you realize your bigger dream?

When the tables were turned and I was asked, I realized my bigger dream at the time was getting my master's degree in journalism. I wanted to validate what I had learned and refine it. I turned my dream into a goal, said it out loud. I did some research and took the first step toward my bigger dream. Never in my wildest imaginations growing up in a northwest Florida fishing village did I see myself going to Harvard University for my master's. Well, I did!

Each of these brave women in *Changing the Rules of Engagement* broadened the scope of opportunities for generations to come by believing their goals were limitless. *It started with a bigger dream and a small step.*

It's only impossible until someone does it.

From writing this book and sharing these stories as a professional speaker, I have also developed my own motto since my retirement from the U.S. Coast Guard:

Be Bold, Be First, Be You!

I can tell you that my bold leadership style empowered me to be one of the first female officers to serve aboard two Coast Guard cutters with all male crews. Patrolling the Pacific and Atlantic Oceans as well as the Caribbean Sea, I remained true to myself while changing the rules of engagement.

Today, as a TEDx and inspirational speaker, I am making a difference using my own "sea stories" and profiles of top leaders, men and women. I believe no matter your age or experience, you can be bold, you can achieve your daring dreams, and you can enjoy the journey of life by being you—being authentic to who you are and where you want to be.

On the topic of being first, there are plenty of ways to be first. It may not be like Nicole Malachowski, who was the first female demonstration fighter pilot for the Thunderbirds, but it most certainly will be along your path toward your bigger dream. There are opportunities to be the first to volunteer to do a job that no one wants to do. Or how about be the first to lead a team on a new project?

Be Bold! I encourage you to not just sit at the table, but rise from the table and take action. Let your voice be heard and work hard, to the best of your abilities, like Mattie Wells.

Be You! Drive toward your goal even if no one looks or thinks like you, like Pam Melroy. And dream your bigger dream; say it out loud and take that first step. You will get there, like me and Heather Wilson.

Be Bold, Be First, Be You!

As I write this following the rise of the pandemic into the new year of 2021, we are witnessing an equalizing climate like never before. Everyone is potentially vulnerable to this coronavirus. We need each other. We need to support each other. To survive we need to work together. We will recover from this and return to our "normal" lives and work routines. How will we have changed from this global experience?

Whether you are a man or woman in the workforce or the military, age, gender, and culture only matter in the sense that we each matter. Our individuality, our diversity, and our teamwork are important to our lives and global success as humans.

We each have a purpose and a place in this world, in this life, to make a difference with our voices and with our best efforts, working hard to the best of our abilities and pursuing our bigger dreams.

If we can appreciate those who don't look, think, or act like us and develop our leadership styles to complement the situations we encounter . . . everyone wins.

Now, let me ask you:

What is one thing you've always wanted to do and haven't done yet?

Say it out loud.

Make it real by articulating it.

Write it down.

Once you do, figure out the steps and then take the first step to get there.

Index

About the Author

Martha LaGuardia-Kotite is an empowerment enthusiast! Ever since she lost her older brother to suicide when she was in high school, she's been motivated to make a difference. Martha does this as a TEDx and inspirational speaker; an author of five books, including the award-winning *So Others May Live: Coast Guard Rescue Swimmers Saving Lives, Defying Death*; and a proud mother and veteran of the U.S. Coast Guard. She is working on her first novel—stay tuned for more news on this!

Be Bold, Be First, Be You: Martha LaGuardia-Kotite's bold leadership style empowered her to be one of the first female officers to serve aboard two Coast Guard cutters with all male crews. Patrolling the Pacific and Atlantic Oceans as well as the Caribbean Sea, Martha remained true to herself while changing the rules of engagement

A graduate of the U.S. Coast Guard Academy with a master's from Harvard University, Martha rose to the senior rank of captain and is an award-winning author of five books. Her leadership presentations are influenced by her twenty-nine-year career serving at sea and ashore and the courageous trailblazers she has profiled in her books.

A senior leader, Martha earned numerous personal and team awards for her mobilizations during national disasters, missions saving lives at sea, and work as a public relations spokesperson. She is nationally dual certified as a National Incident Management System Type I Public Relations Officer and Liaison Officer. She is also certified in ASIST suicide prevention. For additional information about Martha or to request her for an event, please connect with Martha through her website, www.marthakotite.com. Or find her on social media at https://www.linkedin.com/in/marthakotite/ and on Instagram @MKotite.

Additional leadership books by Martha,
which can be found in bookstores and online:

*So Others May Live: Coast Guard Rescue
Swimmers Saving Lives, Defying Death*

Innovators: Rock Stars of STEM

*My Name Is Old Glory:
A Celebration of the Star-Spangled Banner*

CPSIA information can be obtained
at www.ICGtesting.com
Printed in the USA
LVHW030148180321
681773LV00006B/103